SWANAGE
IN WORLD WAR II

SIXTEEN CONTRIBUTIONS

Stewart Borrett

Published by
Amberwood Graphics
34 North Street, Wareham, Dorset BH20 4AQ

ISBN: 978-0-9522281-1-0

Typeset by
Amberwood Graphics, 34 North Street, Wareham, Dorset BH20 4AQ

Printed by
Short Run Press, Exeter, Devon

This book is dedicated to
Neil Millen

Acknowledgements

My thanks go to:

Mike Ford for his help, advice and getting me started.

My editors, Neil Millen who tragically died whilst putting this book together and Brian Withers who took his place.

Ray Holder and Merle Chacksfield.

David Haysom who checked the script through from a historical perspective and for providing photographs from his own collection.

And finally to the contributors themselves who were prepared to be part of this social history of Swanage.

For providing photographs, I gratefully acknowledge:

Neva Errington - Page 11   Eric Gosney - Page 25
Chris Goss - Pages 26, 30   Peter Bunker - Page 27
Dr. Bill Penley - Pages 33, 35, 37, 98
David Haysom - Pages 38, 58, 64, 70, 76
Jim Hunt - Page 41   Molly Wilcox - Page 44
William Lee - Pages 49, 50, 51, 52
Brian Street - Pages 60, 62
Nancy Green - Page 69   Margaret Hughes - Pages 71, 73
Tony Meates - Pages 77, 80, 82
Pat Embleton & Brenda Langdon - Pages 84, 85, 86, 87, 88
Wesley Mullen - 56, 92, 107, 108, 109
Ivan Lock - Page 95   Ray Holder - 104

Pages 36, 100, 105 - Every effort has been made to trace copyright but not known.

Bibliography

'Swanage at War' K. Merle Chacksfield (Swanage Town Council Leisure and Tourism Dept.) 1993

'The British Radar Story 1939-45' Dr. W.H. Penley & R.G. Batt (The Purbeck Radar Museum Trust) 1994

'Luftwaffe Fighter-Bombers over Britain' Chris Goss, with Peter Cornwell and Bernd Rauchbach (Crécy Publishing Ltd.) 2003

Introduction

This book has been produced to give the reader a flavour of Swanage in World War II. It contains sixteen contributions from people who were in Swanage for either the entire war or for only part of it. The contributors range through schoolchildren, evacuees, GIs, a scientist, and a WAAF girl to others who helped keep the town functioning.

What made Swanage so vulnerable was its location on the Channel coast. There was understandably great unease in the town when the German forces overran France in June 1940 and waves of bombers overflew the town on their way to inland targets. But life went on and the true grit and stoicism of the people came to the fore; dances took place, the cinemas were very popular and even the Durlston WI kept meeting!

Schoolchildren had their lives disrupted in September 1939 when 1400 evacuees from London arrived, which in itself caused much chaos. Slit trenches were dug near the schools to be used in case of air raids, and as Mary Green commented, 'You certainly needed your wellington boots'!

Then there was the constant threat of 'tip and run' raids by fighter-bombers from Cherbourg East airfield just seventy five miles away. These took place all across southern England from Truro in Cornwall to the outskirts of London, but coastal towns feared them the most. Swanage as a small town endured four major raids with a total of 20 people killed and 28 seriously injured.

The arrival of hundreds of GIs in November 1943 changed the face of the town: Bill Squibb, who was a schoolboy at the time, thought, 'How could we lose with such a rich and powerful friend'. The GIs were billeted all over the town in hotels, guest houses and any house large enough to take them. They attended dances, sometimes bringing their own bands, drunk the pubs dry, ate food the like of which the local residents had not seen in years, or had never seen; these included powdered eggs, angel cake and Aunt Jemima's spicy fruitcake. The town was now beginning to become more relaxed and positive. I asked one contributor whether the GIs were popular in the town, and he said, "Well I don't know about that, but they certainly had too much money and pinched our girlfriends"!

However the kids loved the GIs, who gave them candies, allowed them to climb up onto their military vehicles, and gorge themselves in their food stations. When the GIs left for the D-Day landings they sent ring donuts to all the schools in the town, so that each child could have one; this was their way of thanking the town.

Contents

Neva Errington

Neva joined the WAAFs in the Midlands and trained as a Radio Telephone Operator. After her training and a period at Middle Wallop, an RAF flying station in Hampshire, she was transferred from there to Swanage to work in an advance station on Studland Hill.

I had to register for war work at eighteen. I was in hairdressing and this obviously wasn't a reserved occupation. I had no desire to work in munitions even though I lived in the Midlands and so many girls were taking up that type of work. A week before I was due to register I travelled to Leicester which was my nearest city, walked into an RAF recruitment office and registered. I was first sent to Innsworth in Gloucestershire for the intake interview and then I was sent to Cardington, the RAF base on the east coast which had housed the fated R101 airship. In the WAAFs I trained as a Radio Telephone Operator and learnt how to operate a '3A panel'. From there I went on to the Air Transport Auxiliary Station in Gosport, and was then transferred to RAF Middle Wallop in Hampshire to finish my training. I was put on shifts, worked in the underground communications room and learnt how to change frequencies.

After I had been there a while it was decided to send some of us to Swanage as Middle Wallop had an advance station on Studland Hill; this was in February 1942. When we were told we were being posted to Swanage none of us had any idea where it was, and we thought we were going to South Wales! There were eight of us and we travelled down in the back of a truck with our kit bags. We arrived late in the evening, there was nobody anywhere on the streets, and we thought 'Gee whizz, what have we come to.' Two of the girls were dropped off at the former military camp area in Ulwell, another two in Redcliffe Road; two more went to Exeter Road, and lastly, we were delivered to a house in Queen's Road called 'Farview'.

Gay Keyser and I were billeted with a private family who provided us with meals. We slept in the two rooms at the very top of the house. We tossed up to see who should have the front bedroom; I lost, and Gay chose the accommodation which had a lovely view over the bay. The man of the house was a teacher and worked over in Wareham, travelling to and fro by train. His wife was considerably younger than he was, and they had three children, one at pre-school and two at the convent school. In their downstairs room at the back there was an Anderson shelter. If the siren sounded in the night the kids didn't like going into the shelter alone, so we went in with them, and played games. They were a lovely family and treated us very well.

The family later moved house, so we transferred to another billet in Mount Pleasant Lane. However this was not suitable and we were only there for a few months. Fortunately our landlady's sister had a flat round the corner above Stan Fordham's, the jewellers, now Corfe Bears, and offered to take us in, so she would have some company while her husband was away fighting in Burma. We went to live with her and stayed there until the war ended.

I worked in an advance station on Studland Hill. There were two RAF units up there, a receiving station where I worked, staffed by WAAFs, and a transmitting station which had all male personnel. The units were positioned there as advance communications for Middle Wallop, which was situated between Salisbury and Andover. When the aircraft took off, Middle Wallop kept in communication with them as far as the coast, and then we would take over while they crossed the channel and into northern France.

Middle Wallop would phone through their operating frequency to us. We then used '3A panels' which were receivers designed to hear communications from the aircraft. We selected a metal plate coding key of the appropriate frequency, inserted it in a slot at the bottom of the panel, and turned the knob until the needle on the dial tuned into the frequency of the aircraft. We then recorded what was going on from their communications with one another, such as their location, speed, direction, whether there was any flak over the target or in the case of fighter aircraft, if they were in a dogfight. All this I wrote down in my log book, which needed to be done quite quickly. We then phoned through the information to the RAF personnel in the transmitting station, which was about 400 yards away. They would then edit the information that had come through, type it out on a teleprinter, and then sent it via a landline to a terminal at Middle Wallop to be printed out.

As far as the facilities we had on the hill were concerned there was an Anderson shelter which was used for storage, and an outside toilet that was primitive to say the least, but we did have electricity and running water. The huts were brick built, about fourteen feet square and were surrounded by an outer blast wall. We operated with quite high aerials which were situated outside. As we entered through the front door, there was a camp bed on the left against the wall: this was used for us to sleep on in rotation when we did night shifts. Straight in front was a bench with the

The footpath to Studland Hill

'3A panels' and on the right, another bench with two telephones.

Gay and I worked together on Studland Hill; there were always two of us working on the shorter shifts. We used bikes to get to work which took about half an hour. We cycled down into town, up Ulwell Road and Redcliffe Road, through to Hill Road and then up the footpath, lifting our bikes over a stile on the way. We then parked them at Whitecliff Farm. From there we would walk up the hill to our hut. We worked a three shift system. Afternoons were from 1 to 6pm, then the next day we would work from 8am to 1pm, and thirdly we returned at 6pm and worked through the night till 8am the following morning. There were three of us on these overnight shifts; one slept on a camp bed while the others worked and then we changed around. We were then free until we started the three shifts again the following day at 1pm, we therefore had a day and a half off, which we certainly needed to catch up on our domestic work, such as washing and ironing.

Some time after we started working on the hill the American Air Force arrived. This occurred when Middle Wallop, which was

Studland Hill Stations

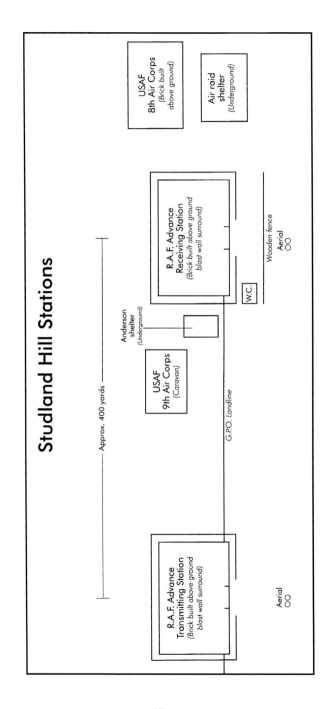

USAF
8th Air Corps
*(Brick built
above ground)*

Air raid
shelter
(Underground)

R.A.F. Advance
Receiving Station
*(Brick built above ground
blast wall surround)*

Wooden fence

Aerial
OO

W.C.

Anderson
shelter
(Underground)

USAF
9th Air Corps
(Caravan)

G.P.O. Landline

Approx. 400 yards

R.A.F. Advance
Transmitting Station
*(Brick built above ground
blast wall surround)*

Aerial
OO

an RAF station, became a joint USAF/RAF station, and their personnel arrived on Studland Hill as an advance station for their aircraft. They were attached to the USAF 8th Air Corps and operated in a brick built hut, like ourselves, on the surface. They had three operators on at any one time, all males and unlike us they came to work by Jeep! They drove up from St. Leonard's, their billet in Rempstone Road, up Ulwell Road towards Studland, then turned right up a track, past where the obelisk is now, up to our RAF transmitting station and parked their Jeep there; however, if it was raining, they drove the whole way! Beside their hut was an underground air raid shelter. On the other side of our hut there was a caravan, which was used by the USAF 9th Air Corps. We used to chat with the guys outside the huts in our breaks, and they would bring along food - donuts, cakes and my favourite, Aunt Jemima's spicy fruitcake. It was, however, quite unusual for us to visit *their* work stations.

We didn't actually visit the RAF personnel in their transmitting station. By the time we had climbed up the hill we didn't feel like doing yet more walking: especially as their station was approximately 400 yards away from ours. The officer who had overall charge of them was Sergeant Elliott who lived in Wyke Lodge in Ulwell Road. One day he said to them "I think I ought to go and have a look at how the girls are getting on because they're on their own". When he arrived I was in the USAF 8th Corps station and was manning their set because they were in the air raid shelter. Their equipment, though it did the same job looked smarter than ours, and the headsets were much more comfortable.

On another occasion the transmitting station was visited by Ivan Lock, a young seventeen year old trainee GPO engineer. He takes up the story, "I went up there on an emergency with my boss. We finished the repair work, he jumped into the van, reversed it round to go back, completely misjudged the gradient and slid halfway down the hill. We then had to walk back into town. By this time people in Swanage were already talking about it because the van was quite visible from the town. We went to the garage in King's Road, which is now the bus depot. During the war this was requisitioned and used as a repair depot for bren gun carriers and

An old GPO map showing Neva's station (top centre) with landline attached. Bay Crescent and Whitecliff Farm bottom right

tracked vehicles. We told them what the problem was, and the officer in charge said "I'll help you out", so he grabbed a bren gun carrier and drove round onto the hill with us, put a rope on our GPO van and pulled it up. Unfortunately it didn't do it much good, and it turned out to be a write-off"!

We WAAFs did socialise with our American colleagues when we were off duty. As mentioned they were billeted at St. Leonard's, a large house in Rempstone Road next to Westbury. Between St. Leonard's and Westbury there was a lawn with quite a sizeable hut standing on it. The Americans used the hut rather like a social club, and we took our records e.g. the Ink Spots round there, did a bit of dancing, and they in turn would serve up soft drinks. They had a great deal of food and drink so it was a pleasant place to relax; the RAF personnel with whom we worked came along as well, as did some local girls.

On other occasions we used to go to dances at the Grand Hotel, in what is now the Burlington Club. The entrance price was around the same as that for the Church Hall in King's Road, about 1/6d. We always wore our WAAF uniforms everywhere; even to a dance; we didn't possess civilian clothes. At the Grand Hotel records were played rather than having a live band and as I recall the dances were on Saturday nights. One particular lady used to come to chaperone her daughter, who was a very pretty girl dressed in civilian clothes. We were all in service uniforms. The Americans were always very keen to chat her up, but Mother kept tight control over her. So when they arrived the Americans used to switch the record to the Jack Buchanan/Elsie Randolph record 'And her mother came too'! I don't think they ever twigged why it was always playing when they arrived. There was masses of food there, mainly because the Grand Hotel was an American food station as well as a billet.

We were always taught to be very wary of the Americans in social situations as a number of them tended to have one thing in mind! At work they would tell us of their conquests the night before, which we all found quite amusing. We service girls were not very popular in Swanage because the local girls thought we were going to take the Americans off them; little did they know we weren't interested as to us they were just work companions and they regarded us in the same way. We felt very sorry for our

English army boys who came into town and even our RAF colleagues, because they simply didn't have the money that the Americans had. Sometimes the American guys we worked with on the hill would go back to Middle Wallop and say to us, "What sort of tobacco does your father like" or "Would your mother like some stockings", as they were visiting their PX up there. The PX was a bit like visiting a supermarket today, and anything one wanted was available. The Americans were so much more liberal than we were and very generous, both to us and to the children in the town.

I met my husband due to Tex, an American I went for a drink with. Tex brought John, my future husband, along with him. John's mother, who was a Swanage woman, lived behind the White Swan pub and had a few rooms there. She used to go into the Services Canteen and one day met Tex Wates who talked about his mother and family back in San Antonio, Texas. She invited him round to her place and he got to know her family.

Tex was a cook, who was billeted along with the others at St. Leonard's in Rempstone Road, and he used to bring her items of food. She mentioned that she wanted to make a Christmas cake but that dried fruit was in very short supply. When Tex heard this he said "Don't worry I'll sort you out something". He went off and brought her back containers of dried fruit, suet, sugar and everything she needed. The 'Snowdrops', (American Military Police) became aware of this practice, and kept a lookout for Americans taking supplies from food stations to give to local people, sometimes for services rendered! Mrs Smith, a woman who lived with John's mother and worked as a cook up at the hospital, heard that the 'Snowdrops' were coming round to peoples' houses to check on food that might have been taken. One day Mrs Smith came running down from the hospital and said "Ma, get rid of all that stuff you were given or they'll send you to prison", so John's mother said "I can't get rid of all this food". So like an idiot she stuffed it all in pillowcases to hide it. Soon, if you came in the front door, the whole place smelt of this dried food fermenting! John's mother said, "If the 'Snowdrops' had come they would have known it was theirs". In fact no-one came round as it was just gossip, and the Christmas cake was made.

A type of dance that was very popular with the Americans was the 'Jitterbug'. We would sometimes go to the dances in the Church Hall in King's Road. There was one WAAF girl who came with us who loved the dance. She was a lovely fresh faced girl with golden hair and she would dance all evening with the guys until her WAAF shirt was soaked in perspiration. I used to say "For goodness sake, how can you get yourself in such a state?". But she really loved the dancing. She used to spend most of her time dancing with one particular American who was very good-looking. Gay and I were going up to London on leave to stay in a hostel. The American guy said to her he was going that weekend to the Locarno in Streatham, and said "Why don't you come up and meet me there". So this girl said to us "If I can get a weekend pass can I come with you". We said "What do you want to come for, we're going to see friends". We tried to warn her that he wouldn't be interested. He was a typical Don Juan type and knew his worth. We knew that his interest in her was merely as a dancer. Anyway we decided to go over to Streatham as well, because we were worried about her; she was only a young kid. Well he was there, dancing away with another girl, and never gave her a second glance, and we knew this would happen. The girl was really heartbroken. We took care of her, and tried to persuade her to understand. When he came back to Swanage we really gave him 'what for', and he got the 'cold shoulder' from all of us. But that's the way life goes.

If we obtained a pass, we quite often went back to Middle Wallop, which required two buses to get there. We went back to see our friends who were on the flying station. At Middle Wallop there was a main control room underground where the operations were monitored. When it was an RAF station the control room was very quiet, and if you wanted to communicate with someone on the other side of the room you spoke quietly by telephone. When the Americans arrived and it was made a joint station, the control room was a very different place. If there was an emergency and their aircraft were being attacked, quite senior ranked officers would get very excited and start running around all over the place, shouting. Seeing this contrast was all very amusing!

When the war ended I returned to Middle Wallop and worked in flying control. I married in January 1946 and was demobbed shortly after. I lived in many places due to my husband's job, but eventually retired to Swanage, and now live a stone's throw away from the house in Queen's Road where I was first billeted, all those years ago.

Eric Gosney

Eric was sixteen and worked at Hardy's the builders when war broke out. He joined the Swanage Air Training Corps' becoming sergeant. When he was twenty in May 1943 he was called up into the RAF to train as a pilot.

The years of 1938-39 were full of rumours of war. Army units were often to be seen around Swanage and one evening my parents spotted two soldiers sitting on our garden wall. They were sergeants Green and Gotobed, in the area on manoeuvres and we invited them in for a meal. Instructions had been given out about air-raid precautions and blackout blinds. Trenches were dug in the field below Mount Scar School; gas masks were fitted and issued and general apprehension felt.

With the outbreak of war many restrictions were applied. The cinemas were closed and other entertainments cancelled for a time. Railings appeared along the beach and concrete pillars called 'Dragon's teeth' were placed along the promenade. Gun emplacements also were built at Peveril Point, the top of the downs and Sandpit Field and there was a good deal of military activity. Rationing began and air-raid precautions were put into force, but no air raids occurred in that first winter while everyone waited breathlessly for what might happen.

Things began to get more exciting in the Spring of 1940, when the Blitzkrieg began with the German invasion of Belgium, Holland and France. Air raids began on British cities and we watched open-mouthed as huge squadrons of enemy aircraft came over the coast on daylight raids, attacked by the RAF. Swanage at this stage of the war was not really a target for enemy bombers. The Germans, however, soon switched their main bombing missions from daylight to night raids and aircraft returning over the coast often dropped bombs at supposed minor targets rather than take them home.

Groups of local businesses combined to form fire-watching groups which might deal with a scattering of incendiary bombs, and so George Hardy's, Robson's Grocery Stores and the Southern Electricity Board premises combined to ensure that their fire-watchers were keeping an eye on their premises. One of Hardy's back offices was provided with tea and soup-making facilities and became the group's headquarters. Duties often lasted for hours on end and working with two other people made the task less onerous and lonely than being on watch alone. It might well be a long vigil, perhaps from 9pm to 6am, and sleeping facilities could not be provided, so a long night was followed by a tiring day at work. Of course, there were long, quiet periods with no aircraft noise when one could play cards or at least stay inside with an occasional foray outside. When the last aircraft had gone out over the coast the 'all-clear' siren was a welcome sound and one was free to go home. I remember being on duty one night when the whistle of a descending bomb was heard. Fortunately it dropped into the sea a hundred yards or so from the promenade and did no damage.

Enemy aircraft were shot down locally and we used to cheer-on the Spitfires and Hurricanes when they broke up enemy formations on daylight raids. A little later 'tip and run' raids occurred - a couple of fighter-bombers would come in over the coast, drop a bomb or two on a fancied target and fly off again.

At the beginning of the war these fighter-bombers were converted Messerschmitt 109s carrying a single bomb, but later the purpose-built Focke-Wulf 190, carrying a single 500kg high explosive bomb was used. They flew in from either Cherbourg East or Caen airfields.

In the summer, bathers would chance their luck and go into the sea between the protective defences. Coming back along the promenade one fine Sunday afternoon I saw two German aircraft climb up over Peveril Point from sea level. I ran into the gents' toilets near the White House and crouched in a corner as I heard the planes flying along the beach, machine gunning. That day, 23rd August 1942, a bomb was dropped on the Swanage Dairies in the Square, demolishing the premises and part of The Ship Hotel.

On another occasion I was arriving home for lunch when aircraft appeared coming in low over Ballard Down and machine gunning. My grandfather was staying with us at that time and mother yelled to him to come into the Morrison shelter in the sitting room, but to no avail. The attack was soon over and we found grandfather still in his chair, quite unmoved. Mother shouted angrily at him, "Why didn't you come to the shelter when I called you"? and he responded, "Well Churchill told us we had to stay put"!

Perhaps my closest shave personally was when a fighter-bomber came in at about six o'clock one evening. I had left Hardy's office and was walking up the High Street, near the Methodist Church, when I heard the sudden, familiar roar of an aeroplane, followed by the sound of machine gunning. I looked around for the nearest cover and ran into Mr Leavis' fruit and vegetable store, near at hand (near where Fusion Hairdressing shop now stands). Not much of a haven really as it was a timber and corrugated iron structure, but I flung myself to the ground inside and, almost immediately, there was a very loud explosion. Dust fell down in clouds all around me from the corrugated iron roof and, as I scrambled to my feet, Mr Leavis also stood up on the other side of the counter. We stared open mouthed at each other for a few seconds, then rushed out into the High Street. A great cloud of dust and smoke hid the Town Hall from sight. "Good God"! I shouted, "They've hit the Town Hall"! Knowing my mother would be concerned for my safety, expecting me home for tea, I hurried up the road and told my story. In actual fact the bomb had demolished Wesley's Cottage, just above the Town Hall. I found myself thinking that, had I left the office a minute later, I would have been, at best, a casualty!

Many lads, like myself, too young to serve in the forces joined service training groups like the Army Cadet Force and the Air Training Corps, while girls joined the Girls Training Corps. It became clear that we should be called up into the services if the war continued as it seemed bound to do. A number of us joined the Air Training Corps when a flight was formed in Swanage: Des Wood, John Dennis, Peter Foote and Vic Simpkins among others. The recruits to the ATC were issued with uniform and met regularly at the Grammar School for instruction of all kinds. We learned navigation from Mr Harry Comben (Head of St. Mark's, Herston) Mr Smith, caretaker at the Grammar School, became our warrant officer and drilled us. We learned Morse code, useful mathematics and other subjects. Our Officer in Charge of the Flight was James

Turner, Headmaster of the Grammar School, who had served in the Royal Flying Corps in World War 1 and flown the Maurice Farman Shorthorn! We were a mixture of Grammar and Council School boys and before long it became necessary to have a boy NCO who would muster the others on parade and take them for a certain amount of drill. No doubt Mr Turner had some headscratching to do, because there were some very able ex-Grammar School boys in the flight, but he diplomatically chose to promote an ex-Council School boy, me! and I was made sergeant. Shortly after this we had to take proficiency tests in mathematics, Morse and navigation and when the results were announced I had come up with the highest marks! Mr Turner congratulated me on parade, smiling as he said, "I see I gave the stripes to the right man, sergeant"!

When we finished our sessions at the Grammar School we came

The Air Training Corps, Swanage Flight.

down into town and made for the Forte's Ice Cream Parlour in the middle of Station Road. There was another cafe we used called Barclay-Bull's, which was at the Square end of The Parade; when Barclay-Bull gave up the cafe it was taken over by a Mrs Grimwood she was great and was very friendly towards us young people.

The ATC was caught up in several interesting activities. One Sunday we marched to St. Edward's church in Corfe Castle for a church parade. We also spent a weekend visiting RAF Warmwell, a fighter station near Dorchester. There we were given short flights in a Tiger Moth training biplane and the first candidate was the Acting Flight Sergeant, myself! Nobody thought to give me the right instructions for the donning of my helmet, goggles and intercom. Consequently my flight was a somewhat strange experience, attempting to hold on to my headgear and not having heard the pilot's information about what he was to do and that he was about to execute a loop. It took me by surprise when my head struck the soft coaming of the cockpit.

Nevertheless it was all very exciting and I straightway determined that I would volunteer for aircrew when the time came.

A Messerschmitt 109 laden with 250kg bomb in Oct 1940.
Four 109s were used in the bombing raid when the
Wesley's Cottage was bombed on 14th May 1941

Peter Bunker

Peter came to Swanage as an evacuee from London. Having escaped the horrors of mass bombing in London's East End he saw wartime Swanage from a child's perspective until the end of hostilities.

Peter in 1949 in the R.A.F. when he was 18

I was born in London's East End and lived at Cemetery Road, Forest Gate, West Ham. I can remember just before the war seeing Sir Oswald Mosley parading with his Nazi sympathisers through the streets with their swastika arm bands, followed by mounted police.

When war was declared on the 3rd September 1939, within minutes of the radio announcement the air raid sirens sounded and we all went into our air raid shelters in the back gardens. However, it was only a practice and we were soon back to normal. Nothing really happened, apart from food becoming short, until after Dunkirk in the spring of 1940 when I was nine years old.

The air raids started in earnest in July, becoming more frequent in August with about seven or eight attacks daily, all at night which necessitated our sleeping on the ground in our Anderson shelter in the back garden.

This continued until September 7th 1940, the worst day of my life. The usual night raids ended around breakfast time and the day started with beautiful sunshine which lasted throughout the day. At about 3pm the sound of aircraft began to be heard, growing louder and louder, the air raid sirens sounded and we all descended into our shelter. From 3.30pm we were bombarded by waves of enemy bombers totalling about one thousand. My sister Sylvia, aged two and a half, and I were screaming with terror. At 6.30pm it ended; both of us were shaking with fear, but then followed the screaming of an aircraft in a dive which missed our house by inches, crashing and exploding in the nearby cemetery. The sky was black with smoke from fires in the Docks and it was said 'one could read a newspaper at midnight by the light thus generated'. From then on we knew what the word 'Blitzkrieg' meant!

On the night of 24th September I was partially awake when there came a number of blinding flashes and several tremendous explosions. I saw our shelter door blown off; this hit the back wall of the house and returned to its original position. This was then struck by what we later discovered to be a large fragment of a bomb casement. Apparently a stick of bombs had fallen in the gardens on the other side of our fence killing an entire family. The rear of our house had gone, as had all the others in adjoining streets. Later in the day, for the first time I saw a man crying and a dog cut in two. People were killing their pets to prevent them from suffering.

My family stored all the furniture that was undamaged inside our house, and on 30th September we left London, with virtually nothing but the clothes we stood up in. I remember changing buses at St.Paul's; all around us was rubble, with the Cathedral standing majestically and almost untouched above the death and carnage below.

Arriving at Waterloo Station we travelled down to Swanage where we had relatives. On the way we saw Southampton was in flames from another pounding on the previous night. I, with my parents, sister, grandparents and an aunt arrived in Swanage and were taken in by our relatives and their neighbours who gave up their beds for us; for the first time in three months we slept in a bed in a house:- this felt like heaven.

We were taken in by the Norman and Crabb families to whom we were related. My father and grandparents were taken in by the Weekes family who lived in the cottages at the bottom of what is now Benleaze Way. Our first night was interrupted by enemy bombers flying overhead, but their target was fortunately not Swanage. My mother said "Eth, hear those planes"? She was promptly told to shut up and go to sleep. The next I knew it was about ten o'clock the following morning.

Although we didn't receive as much bombing at the time compared with London, I was really frightened when air battles raged above us, as we had no air raid shelters, but we soon became used to the Swanage conditions. We managed to rent a house of our own at 1 Victoria Terrace, Jubilee Road, next door to a lovely young girl whom I took a liking to; her name was Joan Dorey. As we had no furniture at the time, the secondhand shops supplied us with the basics, but the people of Herston were very kind to us, giving us chairs, a table and crockery. Later, we recovered some undamaged furniture from London.

Early in 1941 my father was called up into the R.A.F. Later that year in October my Grandmother died and on the day of the funeral Sylvia and I were cared for by two elderly ladies at Newton Cottage in the High Street. On 23rd August 1942 Newton Cottage was destroyed in a bombing raid and the occupant Joe Hibbs, who was in the house at the time, later died from his injuries.

Some weeks later my mother, grandfather, aunt, cousin and

sister Sylvia walked to Godlingston to tend my grandmother's grave. They had just arrived in the field where the footpath commences when, without warning, two Focke-Wulf 190s attacked, one of which sprayed machine gun bullets around the family group, and shortly after there was an explosion in one of the gasholders behind. Seeing that there was a second plane coming in, my Grandfather pushed everyone into a ditch as it strafed the ground with yet more machine gun fire. Afterwards it was found that the ground on which they had been standing seconds before, was peppered with bullets and would have wiped them all out, but for my grandfather's quick thinking. Fortunately I was elsewhere at the time.

Two Focke-Wulf 190s wait to take off on another bombing raid into Southern England

In Swanage my closest shave came when my friend Brian Clarke and I were on our way to the 'Cinema'. We walked past the bottom of Spring Hill, and I suppose it would have taken us about a minute to walk from there to the 'Cinema'. As we went up the steps into the auditorium there was an terrific explosion, with windows shattering and ceilings falling on us. Two usherettes grabbed us and pushed us into the box office, throwing themselves on top of us. The bomb scored a direct hit on the house at the bottom of Spring Hill, where we had been one minute before, killing Mrs Swaine and others in the house. If this wasn't fate I don't know what was!

On 3rd February 1943 several Focke-Wulf 190s attacked the

town. One bomb hit the Congregational Church at the apex of the south wall, passed through it taking out the north wall, and in the process destroying the organ. The bomb exploded in the small cemetery near the Rectory Classroom, blowing out priceless stained glass windows in the Parish Church and taking off the roof. The inside of the Church was in a sorry state, deep in debris, which made it too dangerous to hold services there for a while. Some temporary repairs were made to the roof and windows to render them waterproof. On 21st March, services resumed in St. Mary's and on that day I joined the choir.

The American Army arrived in November 1943 and, soon afterwards, I can vividly remember three GIs in full battle gear standing at the bottom of Jubilee Road handing out candy, oranges, and bananas the like of which we hadn't seen for years. When I was at St. Mary's Church one Sunday eight black GIs joined us for Matins, two of whom climbed up the flagpole after the service to unravel the flag. Mr Goodey the Verger wanted Michael Gifford and myself to do this, and we were greatly relieved that we were rescued from this task. Around this time we occasionally had sermons from some American Army Clergy, one of which referred to Swanage as a 'city' which caused much amusement to us choirboys.

My family became friendly with an American Clergy Captain by the name of Captain Andrews, we were told to call him Padre. He was friendly with a young female relative of ours. Two days before D-Day I was in the High Street at Herston watching a large convoy of troops coming into Swanage. Suddenly our Padre stood up in his Jeep and shouted "Hi Pete, goodbye and God bless you all". That was the last I ever saw of him, which still makes me feel quite emotional after all these years.

The afternoon before D-Day we were coming out of St. Mark's School when someone shouted "Down the seafront quickly!"; when we arrived the whole area was covered in ships and it was said that one could walk to the Isle of Wight without getting one's feet wet. That night we had no sleep as waves of aircraft flew low over our roof tops. We knew finally, after having to put up with being attacked for four and a half years that the boot was firmly on the other foot at last.

On the morning of D-Day itself the skies were full of our aircraft, some coming back with smoke streaming from them, their crews hoping to make it to the RAF station at Tarrant Rushton. With all the GIs gone, Swanage became very quiet until September 1944, when the allies had obtained a firm hold in France and some of the American 1st Division returned on leave.

One evening a GI asked a few of us to take him to the Churchill family in Steer Road. Janet Churchill had married Sgt. Donald McAllister who was killed at Caumont in Normandy. On the way we asked him what it was like on the beaches, he replied "You kids have seen enough war here:- you don't need to know any more". We hid in the hedge as he knocked on the door and asked to go in. Then we walked quietly away.

Mixing with these young American lads, some of which were only nineteen, we could clearly see that they had completely changed since we first met them in late 1943. They were very quiet and subdued after what they had endured on Omaha beach and beyond in Normandy.

Leaving politics aside, I've always had a great deal of time for our American friends whom I found to be very generous and loyal, and very good friends both during the war and later while I was on my National Service at the RAF/USAF base at Mildenhall in Suffolk.

Dr. Bill Penley

Bill came to Swanage in May 1940 from Dundee where he worked on radar. The development of radar had started at Orfordness in 1935 and a chain of stations was being set up from Scotland down the East and the South coasts to Worth. The team had been evacuated to Dundee at the start of the war but this remoteness was unsatisfactory so the main group of two hundred people was told to move to new buildings being built at Worth.

Bill Penley in 1943

On the 9th May 1940 Alex Cowie and I were having breakfast at Barclay-Bull's Guest House, No. 1 The Parade, with two girls from the Maths group after having travelled overnight by train from Dundee. We needed accommodation and the girls had been given some addresses. One was 192 King's Road West so Alex and I went to have a look with them. The girls were suited there with a Mr Collier who was a hairdresser in Station Road. He mentioned that next door Mr and Mrs Howe, who were boarding house people, would probably like to accommodate us; this indeed happened, so we were given the front room and two bedrooms. Mrs Howe provided us with breakfast, sandwiches to take up to work and an evening meal. We stayed at 194 King's Road for a year and a half. Other staff went into the Wolfeton Hotel, Craig-y-Don, other hotels and guest houses or, like us, digs. A few senior staff rented houses.

An initial chain of radar stations had been set up around London in 1936 and following successful trials in 1937 it was decided to extend it round the coast from the Isle of Wight to the Tay. These stations had been developed to detect incoming high flying aircraft over 100 miles away. This was to enable our daytime fighters to remain on the ground until formations of bombers were located; the fighters could then be scrambled and directed to the best places to intercept them.

It was also known that, with the transmission pattern we were deploying, bomber aircraft would be able to sneak in under the radar cover. To overcome this you needed higher frequency equipments put on higher platforms, so Dennis Taylor, John Duckworth and myself were put to work on these lower angles radar in Dundee. They were called 'Coast Home Low' stations (CHLs). One of these was placed near Renscombe Farm at Worth but did not work effectively so far inland. We put one on the cliff at St. Alban's Head and showed that a high cliff site was excellent.

With the threat of invasion we went round the chain stations to make them work properly and when raids increased the whole setup enabled the small band of fighters to prevent the enemy from gaining air superiority. The initial Battle of Britain had been won. With so few fighters this was only possible due to radar.

Towards the end of 1940 Goering changed to night bombing raids and we had to develop new equipment based on the CHL design to meet this threat. The installation we set up at Sopley was very effective and HM the King saw a successful interception in May 1941.

After a year and a half at King's Road John Duckworth found a flat at No.11 The Parade and we moved in. The building was owned by Mrs Barnaby, who lived on the main floor. The top two floors were available and had a separate entrance with a key. We were treated like lords. Mrs Barnaby had two maids living in the basement who cleaned our rooms. We provided the food and our meals were cooked for us completely free - we just paid for the rooms, so we had a fine time.

We used to go swimming from the flat. We walked past the old Mowlem Institute, climbed through the circular metal tubing which acted as part of the beach defences, and swam out to sea.

The other activity I loved was singing. Before arriving in Swanage I had almost taken up singing as a career. I ran a quartet when I was younger and sang in the cathedral choir at Dundee. In Swanage I started a small singing group of both sexes, some of whom were trained singers. There were about ten or twelve members from the Radar Establishment so we had a nice little group . We met in the Albany Rooms in Town Hall Lane, which were owned by Mr Klitz who ran the music shop over the road in the High Street. You walked up some steps to a room with a piano on the first floor . We used to meet once a week and sing motets and things of that kind.

When we moved down to Worth all functions of the Establishment were there: administration, workshops, drawing offices, labs, but there were only about two hundred members of staff. We obtained priority for recruiting the top scientists and

Leeson House

engineers in the country for this work and in the two years we were here this increased to over two thousand. As the top teams came in and started to do work on the centimetric frequencies we built more huts, but it became clear that we were bursting at the seams. So it was decided to requisition Durnford School in Langton and set it up as the administration centre. So the superintendent and most of the senior staff, such as W.B. Lewis in charge of the research programme, all moved their offices to Durnford.

When work got going on centimetric radar and the magnetron was invented, this work was moved to Leeson House, which was also requisitioned. So Drs. Dee, Skinner, Lovell and Hodgkin, the early workers on the centimetric air interception radar, moved down to Leeson. Joan Curran was a scientist who had joined the team working under Bob Cockburn; 'Windows' was the code name for the aluminium strips developed there. These were used to confuse the German radar activities. Jamming was used to confuse their bombing beams. His team took a leading part in planning the spoof raid for D-Day.

Joan Curran producing the
aluminium strips

It became clear that a rapid increase in the number of trained people was essential in order to get a worthwhile operation out of these rather crude equipments, and to maintain them. So Forres was taken over to be used as a training school for RAF radar operators and maintenance technicians.

Taffy Bowen & Prof. Hanbury-Brown having lunch at the Square and Compass

In May 1942, after two years, the time came to leave. I was a section leader and we were called down to Durnford House to hear an announcement from the Superintendent Jimmy Rowe. He told us that Winston Churchill had ordered us to leave by the next full moon. Intelligence reports indicated that a large force was being prepared at Cherbourg and it was felt that this might be a threat to the Establishment, so the decision was made to leave.

Pickfords had been requisitioned to take the equipment away and we were given a time and date to depart for Malvern in Worcestershire. Before that a few of us who had teams to organize had been up to Malvern Boys College to see our working area, and to mark up the plans of the rooms we were allocated for benches, power and telephones. The Admiralty had prepared these plans because The College had been chosen as a place for them to go if they had to leave London in a hurry.

But on the day of the proposed move there was a glitch. John Duckworth and I had to go over to where the Studland Road joins the main road the other side of Corfe, to form a cordon and turn people back, "Not today, tomorrow". How they managed it I don't know, it must have been a hell of a business.

When we finally left I went up with John Duckworth who had recently bought an old Morris car. We made our way up to Malvern on our own and were unwelcome visitors allocated 'shelter billets'; there was no food or even anywhere to dry our wet clothes, it was ridiculous. After living like lords on The Parade in Swanage we certainly came down to earth.

The 'Dragon's teeth' as part of the beach defences, 1945

Jim Hunt

Jim was a catholic schoolboy during the war and he gives a clear account of what it was like growing up at that time. He joined the Sea Cadets and, when the Americans arrived in November 1943, became actively involved with them, selling them papers, having breakfast at their billet and receiving their K rations.

As a schoolboy I attended St. Joseph's Catholic School in Chapel Lane. Father Corr was the Parish Priest and town councillor, he campaigned to set up St. Joseph's which was the first Catholic school in the town.

I remember very clearly the outbreak of war. I was serving at the 11am mass along with my brother Kenny. Father Corr was well into his sermon when his housekeeper, Miss Marshall came up to the altar and handed him a note which stated that Neville Chamberlain had declared war on Germany. Father Corr was very upset as he had served in France during the First World War and had witnessed the horrors that such a conflict could bring.

After that day, 3rd September 1939, our school life changed dramatically. The school windows were blacked out and netting was fixed to the ceilings to help prevent debris falling on us if the building was bombed. The authorities issued all children with gasmasks which they had to take to school with them.

In those days there was a stone bridge crossing over Chapel Lane from our playing fields into a field which is now Queens Mead. Hayter's the builders dug six lanes of trenches in that field and, when the air raid warning sounded the children from St. Joseph's shared these with the pupils from Mount Scar School. I well remember watching a dogfight over Swanage in which an RAF Spitfire shot down a German bomber which crash landed at Studland. With the Luftwaffe bombing raids on southern England getting worse, we had to move out of St. Joseph's and go into makeshift classrooms beside the convent.

St. Joseph's was taken over by a catholic school from Southampton. Our school lessons were frequently disrupted by the air raid siren which was located on the roof of the Town Hall.

On hearing the siren, we had to pick up our gasmasks and walk, not run, in an orderly manner, across the courtyard to the cellar in the convent. At the top of cellar steps stood the Reverend Mother with a little bowl of holy water with which we had to bless ourselves before descending these thirteen steep stone steps into the cellar. The high school girls from St. Mary's in their pale blue uniforms were already sitting at the widest part of the cellar. We were kept well away from them by the figure of Sister Mary Oswald who stood facing us with her arms folded!

For a small town Swanage had its quota of bombings. I remember when bombs fell and destroyed buildings on Chapel Lane just beside our school and another bomb destroyed Wesley's Cottage opposite the convent. It was at this time that the people of Swanage warmed to the nuns for their kindness, as they took in bombed-out people and shared their rationed meals with them.

During the Battle of Britain we had air raid warnings almost every night as well as during the day. The authorities advised people who did not possess outdoor Anderson shelters to use their coal cellars during air raids, as the walls were thicker. I remember my mother covering the coal with sacks so that my brother, sister and I, together with my mother and two pets, one cat and one dog, could sit there during an air raid. Very often we could hear the noise of enemy bombers passing over Swanage on their way to bomb the Bristol docks. All the ack-ack guns in and around Swanage would often fire on them and on occasions some of the bombers would indiscriminately drop their bombs. I remember how frightened we were at night when we heard the screaming, whistling noise that the bombs made as they fell and how we waited for the terrible noise as they exploded.

Later on in the war, all homes were supplied with steel indoor table shelters called Morrison shelters. We used them as dining tables, games tables etc. whilst underneath was our bedding where we would sleep.

My father was away from home working for the Air Ministry, but when he was at home, he was required to do compulsory night-time fire watching duties out on the streets. He used to wear a steel helmet to protect his head from falling shrapnel that came from the ack-ack barrage of exploding shells.

I remember one particular night very well, there had been a heavy bombing raid over Poole. The siren had sounded the all-clear and we were just settling down for a little sleep before getting up for school when my father came in from fire watching duties and told us to get up and dress. We had to leave our home immediately as a time bomb had landed nearby. As we left our home and went out into the cold night air we saw many others being evacuated as well. Our homes were cordoned off and we were taken to the house of Mr & Mrs Len Bradford, who had offered to take us in. We stayed with them for three nights and they and their children shared their rations with us, as what food we had was back in our house, along with our ration books. I shall never forget the kindness shown to us by the Bradford family.

Almost every day we would hear of another serviceman, either wounded, missing, killed or taken prisoner. So when we were children the war was our life and all we knew.

Colonel Russell heading a Sea Cadet Corps parade

My brother Kenny and I, along with other young boys, were part of the Sea Cadet Corps and our headquarters was above what is now K's amusement arcade. The naval officer running the Sea Cadets at Swanage was an ex-army colonel, Colonel Russell. He was very much like Captain Mainwaring from Dad's Army and very strict on discipline. The other officer in charge was Mr Butler who was the headmaster at St. Mark's School at Herston. He served in the Navy during the First World War.

In the Sea Cadets we were taught seamanship, Morse code, semaphore signals, which was a system of sending messages by holding flags in certain positions, and how to tie knots. We had lots of drill with Colonel Russell, with his monocle in one eye, shouting at us to keep in step. We had a sailing yacht named 'The Jane' that was moored off Buck Shore to which we rowed out, in a dinghy; we had to make sure we didn't get shouted at if we 'caught a crab' with the oars. Sometimes we would get a clip round the ear for not letting go of the jib sail quickly enough.

In November 1943, we thought God had sent us help with the arrival in Swanage of the 26th Regiment of the American 1st Division, known as the 'Big Red One'. Many hotels and large houses were requisitioned. The Yanks were very much liked by the Swanage people for their friendliness, good behaviour and generosity, especially to us children. They laid on a big Christmas party at the Church Hall in Kings Road for the children, and we tasted food that we had not seen for ages. David Sparkes, my brother Kenny and I sold newspapers to the young soldiers in their billet at the Craigside Hotel in the mornings before going to school. Some of them would let us borrow their mess kits to join the breakfast queue. Some also give us their K rations which contained food that we had never seen because of the severe rationing. The K ration was a waxed box containing biscuits, chocolate, small cans of ham, eggs, orange and lemon powder, candy, chewing gum and cigarettes. We got very friendly with the cook there who was known as 'Two Gun'. They loved talking to us kids; they were homesick, and they would tell us all about their families and life as it was, back in the States.

The cinema in Station Road was full of GIs every night and the pubs soon ran dry once they arrived. Gracie's Cafe, which was just over the road from the cinema was also very popular with them. Regular dances were also held at the Church Hall and the GIs taught the local girls to Jive and Jitterbug. There were many love affairs in Swanage during 1943 and 1944 and many local girls married GIs, resulting in children and grandchildren.

As many of the Americans were catholic, they had their own RC chaplain and also had their own services in our church, but many came also to our services. I remember serving on the Altar during Christmas 1943 and looking down the church and seeing all those men in khaki uniforms, who outnumbered our own local parishioners. The whole congregation sang the lovely carol, 'Adeste Fideles', which in those days was sung in Latin in catholic churches. I shall never forget how beautifully it was sung, and every Christmas when I hear that carol in our church I remember those far-off days.

I also remember, along with other boys, trying to see past sentries guarding Swanage Railway Station. We managed to see the three special trains standing in the station and goods yard. One belonged to King George VI, one to General Montgomery and the third to General Eisenhower. They had all travelled down to Swanage to review the full-scale rehearsals at Studland in preparation for the Normandy landings.

I stood behind Canadian soldiers on guard with fixed bayonets on both sides of Station Road, and saw King George VI drive past to the cheers of onlookers.

Soon afterwards the friendly young GIs, who were so much part of everyone's life here in Swanage during that cold winter of 1943/44, left. Many of them were to die on Omaha Beach in the D-Day landings in June 1944. We owe such a debt to those GIs, who along with our own men and women made such a sacrifice for the liberation of Europe.

Molly Wilcox

Molly came from a Swanage family and after leaving school at fourteen went to work at the New Era Cleaners in The Square. She worked there for the duration of the war taking in military uniforms as well as doing other voluntary work.

When war broke out we were living at 84 Kings Road which was next door to a florists shop. I was born in 1918 and was the youngest of eight children, my mum being in her 40s when I was born. My eldest sister Dorothy was 20 years older than I was, and she was married and lived away from Swanage. There was Gerald, Phyllis, Tom, Jack, and Marjorie who married and lived in Corfe Castle, while the other two had married and left Swanage. Phyllis and myself were the only ones living at home during the war.

I remember I used to sleep at home on a single mattress under the stairs; I felt very safe doing this and that nothing untoward would happen to me. Waves of bombers were coming over Swanage at that time, and when we were caught in town we sheltered in the basement of Sydenham's, a gents' outfitters in Institute Road. Around this time I went on a visit with my sister to London where there was no bombing at all.

For the duration of the war I worked at the New Era Cleaners which was located at 10 The Square, where Rainbow's End Too is now. I'd started working at the cleaners straight from school when I was fourteen. The headquarters and laundry were located at Pokesdown in Bournemouth. Mr Bell and Mr Waters were the owners, and these were the people we contacted if anything went wrong. The other girl I worked with in the shop was called Betty Norman: I remained good friends with her for over seventy years. She was a lovely person and always had a smile on her face. We had no manager present in the shop so Betty and I just 'got on with it'. Occasionally Mr Waters would turn up, unexpectedly, probably to check we were not skiving, but basically we were on our own and if there were any problems we phoned them or they phoned us.

During the war nothing was done on the premises. Before the war, steam pressing was carried out here by a man called George, but when he was called up, even that was done at Pokesdown. The van came over once a day to collect all the dirties which were put in black sacks, every item of which had to be marked. We didn't know when the van was going to arrive as it went round to collect from other places. Laundry items such as sheets were washed and the clothes were dry-cleaned with chemicals. Once Pokesdown had done their work the cleaned articles were neatly folded, placed in hampers and sent back to Swanage by rail. They were then transferred to a railway delivery van and brought back to us. We then had to individually wrap them. Occasionally cleaned items came back on the daily van but not very often as there was no room; this was because dirties were collected from other addresses.

We worked six days a week with Sunday as our day off, and

Thursday was a half day. Our hours during the war were 8.30 to about 5; we basically went home when it became dark in the winter, and this 5pm finish still applied in summer. We had an hour for lunch with the shop closing between 1 and 2pm. One of the pleasant things about this job was that we were our own bosses and never had a manager supervising us. I believe at this time I was earning about 10/6d a week.

When we arrived at work the first thing we used to do was sweep out the shop and wash down the pavement outside. When a suit was brought in we had to sew a tag on each item, waistcoat, trousers and jacket. For this a long marking tape was used with 'S' for Swanage and a number; moreover if the garment needed to be shortened, for example four inches, all that had to be written on the tape. Sometimes soldiers came down from the Durlston Court with garments. We never wrote the tapes until we had finished work on the item in hand; sometimes when we had finished the work we'd forgotten the name of the person who had brought it in, so we simply used to make up a fictitious name and hope it would all work out! When we were really busy it was a nightmare remembering everything.

The uniforms that came in were dry cleaned using the chemical carbon tetrachloride. If they had been washed in water the uniforms would have shrunk once dried. We had a great many well-to-do people using the shop, debutantes used to bring in their evening dresses with long gloves. We even used to mend ladies' stockings. Some of the regular customers I remember were the Yoes, Harry Warren House in Studland, the Tadmans' at Langton, (he was the vicar), the Chadwicks' from Forres School, the Hicksons' who ran Oldfeld School; many of them had accounts. At the other end of the social spectrum there were people who asked us to dye blankets which were then made into clothes; some people had to do this because of the clothes rationing.

The work was probably divided equally during the war, between military uniforms and private work. There were situations where individual service people would bring in their uniforms and other occasions when a hundred were brought all at once, probably by a regiment. We took the money and wrote the amount down on a till roll, recording the order number and amount taken. We didn't have a mechanised keyboard till, just a simple wooden one. I had to cash up at the end of the day and check it against what had been written on the till roll. I also had to do the weekly returns, this work I often I did on a Sunday, to try and make it balance. In addition, a list had to be made of all the parcels left in the shop.

On one occasion a serviceman came in and said he was going on leave and wanted his battledress cleaned by a certain day. I phoned Pokesdown and said, "Can you guarantee to have the uniform ready by a certain time"; they replied, "Yes that will be fine". Well, needless to say it didn't arrive when it was supposed to; Pokedown said it had been sent on the train. The railway van had delivered for that day, and deliveries used to arrive at any time. I felt so sorry for the soldier because I promised it would be ready. I therefore contacted the railway station and asked if I could come up and open the hamper, remove the particular battledress and bring it back to the shop to pack up. Fortunately they agreed and after I had removed the uniform I fastened the hamper back up again to be delivered the next day. The serviceman lived at Studland, so I hitched a ride there on the early morning mail van, walked down to Knoll House, delivered the battledress and collected the payment. There were two companies that delivered to Studland, namely King's and Lovelace's, so I came back on one of the vans. I did this because I really felt for this soldier, as he wanted to go back home with a clean battledress. It often happened that we said to people in the shop, "Oh yes, that will be fine it'll be back in time", and then it didn't turn up, I always felt so bad when they came back to pick up their cleaning and found it had not arrived.

The 'Services Canteen', located in the Trocadero building was asking for volunteers so Betty and myself went to work there two evenings a week, Mondays and Fridays. We worked from 7 to 11pm. On the Monday we worked in the kitchen. We didn't cook but served up snack type meals at the hatch, such as cheese on toast. On Friday we were waitresses, so we shouted our orders down the hatch and took them round to the tables. Anyone who was in uniform could go to the 'Services Canteen', males or females, and also the foreign troops, Americans and Canadians. It was incredibly well patronised and was a relaxed place to work; we didn't have to wear a uniform, just anything that was smart. I worked there for quite a number of the war years.

Another wartime community activity I got involved in was firewatching. All the businesses around the Square used to get together and organise a rota. There were Betty and myself, the housekeeper from Vye's the butcher's shop on the corner of Stafford Road, Miss Mills who worked in the Home & Colonial shop, the manager of Robson's, and Mr Cann who worked at the Town Hall. We used to operate from two rooms at the top floor of what is now the Sue Ryder shop in Institute Road. We had camp beds there and sometimes slept over and went home the following morning at about 8am. As far as I remember we were never called out, except to do our initial training which we did in the Rectory Classroom. The general idea was to go out if any incendiary bombs were dropped and then report it to the appropriate authority. My boyfriend was in the army at the time and when he came home on leave I took some time off from firewatching:- ironically enough, this was the only time they were called out!

In what little leisure time I did have I liked going to the cinema very much and on my half day a number of us girls went out for walks; one of them lived at Blacklands an area of Acton, so we caught the bus up there and walked from there down to Chapman's Pool. We would take a picnic and then walk back to the girl's cottage to have a meal. We also used to walk over the hill to Studland some evenings and take our supper with us.

In our family we basically had to make do with the food rations we had and we didn't manage to get too much extra. I remember watching out for the Walls ice cream van that came down to Bruce Hibbs, a grocery store at the bottom of Park Road where Jenkins is now. If I spotted him from the shop I contacted mum and she used to come down and buy some; this was a real luxury.

I eventually left the New Era Cleaners in 1948, after sixteen years service to start a family.

William Lee

Bill arrived in Swanage in November 1943 as a GI with the US Army 1st Infantry Division better known as the 'Big Red One'. He stayed seven months, billeted at the Royal Victoria Hotel, until leaving to take part in the D-Day landings in France.

I arrived in England, docking at Glasgow, after a long sea voyage from Palermo in Sicily. We were placed on a troop train and arrived at Wareham on November 7th 1943, then trucked to Swanage.

I was part of 'D' Company, 26th Infantry, US 1st Infantry Division. This was a heavy weapons company manning 30 calibre machine guns and 81mm mortars. We were dispatched to rifle companies to add firepower to their smaller calibre weapons.

Bill by his window at the Royal Victoria Hotel

There were about 250 of us in 'D' Company and we were all billeted at the Royal Victoria Hotel. The 'Royal Vic' was austere and in disrepair and we slept on the floor on mattresses filled with straw. I had the 'Grand Suite' and shared it with about 20 other GIs. We had a ground-floor room, which fronted on to Seymer Road and looked over towards the Downs. There were no bars, or anything in the way of niceties - this was strictly a billeting establishment. Our kitchen area was in the front of the Hotel. We walked in a single file past the cooks who would place the food in our mess kit. All our food was shipped over from the States and prepared on site. We had a variety of food such as ham, potatoes, beans of various kinds, coffee or iced tea etc. Breakfast might be ham and gravy or even once in a while pancakes made while we waited; it varied a lot, but I do remember we had some kind of fruit every day.

Bill's buddy Stanley Yorz

The Hotel was taken over while we were there by the US military and no English folk were allowed into our area. However I do remember small boys coming to sell us their papers after their folks had read them, and they had pressed them with an iron!

During the war the two hotels the Royal Victoria and the Grosvenor were run by the same Exton group. However the Grosvenor was quite a different sort of establishment, for the officers. I only went up there once when a friend of mine from my home town visited me, and we met up there. I felt quite ill at ease with my officers, I slipped out as quickly as I could - this was not for me!

The 'Big Red One' was in England for the express purpose of invading France and we trained every weekday from November 1943 to May 1944. During our training we would go on long hikes up to 20 miles and I remember the whole regiment one day hiked to Stonehenge.

We also trained in simulated landings to prepare us for D-Day. In one simulation German E-Boats caught the landing parties by surprise - we lost heavily in this raid, but no one heard about the disaster until well after the war was over.

On another training day we were supported by a tank from our unit. We were going down the High Street when a tank hit the front of a store or pub. This caused quite a disturbance, a crowd formed and the training day was somewhat delayed by the collision. I'm not sure what happened afterwards but no doubt the US Government had to pay damages.

Bill's view overlooking Seymer Road towards the pig grazing area

One day we were around the 'Royal Vic' when a Spitfire returned, no doubt after an attack over the channel and all of a sudden the pilot parachuted from the plane; we later heard he had been killed. However the Spitfire continued on its way and landed with very little damage. Strange thing, plane came home safely, but the pilot was lost, the fortunes of war.

At the weekends passes were usually issued and you could travel to any place provided you returned by morning check on a Monday. When I got a pass over the weekend I would usually take off to London with another soldier and go to the movies or sights in the capital. We travelled by trains and buses or anything else that was available, though we never used military vehicles. Every month while in England we were paid by our forces in pounds Sterling so this enabled us to get around a bit. We stayed in accommodation made available to soldiers by the Red Cross.

We, as GIs, were provided with a leaflet about how to behave and treat the indigenous population. We were encouraged to visit English families and were reminded to always take food items to supplement their rationing. In light of this many English families would seek to have soldiers visit them and we took various foodstuffs, coffee, sugar, lard, fruit etc. I visited a family near Bovington Camp and remember giving them some lard and a bag of sugar. Many GIs stationed in Swanage used to go over to Bovington Camp for dances.

As mentioned, we were provided with fruit every day. I remember sharing my fruit with two small girls, Margaret Pole and Hazel Cotthead, who were about 8 or 9 years old at the time.

Hazel and Margaret, February 1944

They came to my window at the 'Royal Vic' and had never seen oranges before so it was nice to give them a treat; they reminded me of my nieces back in the States.

My stay in England was the best time of my army service. 'The folks' spoke English though slightly differently from our speech. I had great admiration for the English who had endured hardships us Americans hadn't known, as we had arrived late! I remember us

GIs would go to a pub and in five minutes drink up the beer ration for the week. Perhaps that was one thing the English didn't like about the 'bloody yanks'. We hadn't known about the queues the English used, with us it was 'first come first served'. We finally learned to queue, and I believe our English cousins forgave us for our uncouth manners.

When the war ended I had spent 37 months overseas in combat; in 8 major campaigns, and had not seen home in all that time. But I survived.

Bob Dwen

Bob came to Swanage as an evacuee from Southampton. Upon leaving school he went to work at Dunesby's, a greengrocers in Station Road, as well as working as a messenger boy for the Air Raid Precautions Service. He later worked as a projectionist at the 'Cinema'.

I lived with my family in Newcombe Road in Southampton, and was one of nine children. Before the war my father had been a professional soldier and when war was declared he was called up. On the Thursday before war was declared on the Sunday, I was evacuated to Parkstone and we were enrolled in the Branksome Hall School. There were no classrooms, just an open hall. The classes were divided into groups and since they were so close to one another, if you were not interested in your lesson you could always listen to another. After about five months, because things were so quiet with no activity, most of us children returned to Southampton.

Things soon warmed up. One Saturday dinner time my mother had just put the meal on the table when without warning a bomb dropped in the next road. The blast blew out our front windows and the front door, while the ceiling came down on our dinner. Five of my sisters and my brother were in the front room. They were unhurt but the door was jammed and it took us about ten minutes to rescue them whereupon we all rushed to the shelter. We remained there all afternoon and the following night until the all clear sounded at 8am the next morning. We had had nothing to eat or drink since breakfast the day before.

One night shortly after this ordeal the sirens sounded again, and we rushed to the shelter. When we reached it my mother found she had left behind her handbag which contained all her policies. She asked me to return to the house and retrieve it. I was scared stiff; there were so many looters around at the time that the army had been instructed to shoot on sight. I never saw a soul on the way and soon arrived at the house; I had to use the back door as the front was nailed up. In the darkness I found the handbag, then safely returned to the shelter. It was a brilliant clear night with a full moon and, as I reached the shelter, I saw a parachute coming down. I pointed this out to the A.R.P. Warden and he shouted "Get to the shelter quick!" Just as I gave my mother her bag there was a terrific explosion and the ground shook. Some of the women started screaming. It turned out to be a landmine, which landed on the convent next to my school. As a result of this several of the nuns were killed.

It was due to these awful events that two weeks later we were re-evacuated to Swanage. I was taken in by Billy Baker and his wife; Billy worked as a taxi owner/driver and was very happy there. One day he called us out into the garden where we watched the vapour trails from a dogfight above; the sound of the cannon fire could clearly be heard. One of my sisters was evacuated with me, and she went to live with Mrs Churchill in the High Street at Herston.

It then quietened down in Southampton again so some of us returned home once more. However it was only a month later that the heavy raids began, so once again I was shipped off to Swanage. This time I was billeted with Mrs Bolson in the High Street. As our house in Southampton was so badly damaged my mother decided to come to Swanage and rent a room whilst looking for a house for us all to live in. Fortunately one which was called 'Mimi Lake' became available in King's Road East and so she made her home here for the duration of the war. Later we moved to a house in Stafford Road, which was rented as had been the first.

I left school at Christmas 1941 and went to work at Dunesby's the greengrocers in Station Road. When Swanage started to experience bombing itself, Bill Dunesby told me that the Air Raid Precautions Service needed messengers, and he encouraged me to do this in addition to continuing my work with him. To do this A.R.P. work, the main prerequisite was the possession of a bicycle. In the beginning I was the only messenger that was recruited. My work consisted of reporting to the A.R.P. Report Centre at 'Dunoon' in Rabling Road when the air raid siren sounded. I was then given messages which I delivered to the relevant rescue parties.

My first encounter, ironically enough, turned out to be the worst raid of the war on the 17th August 1942 which involved the bombing of the Westminster Bank. I had just finished work for the day, rushed to the Report Centre and was given a message for the rescue party around 5.30pm. There was nothing left of the bank and I watched as they dug out the body of Mr Mills, the manager. He had been down in the vault and the whole building collapsed on him. There were no obvious signs of injury and he looked as though he was asleep. I never saw anyone else who had been killed. During this raid I learnt that eight people died and eleven were seriously injured.

The next incident occurred on the 23rd August when two Focke-Wulf 190s came in around 5pm and fired their cannons at the gasworks in Victoria Ave. Once again I was given a message to deliver to the officer in charge. When I arrived the army personnel were up on the gantry trying to extinguish the flames which were coming out of the bullet holes. They did a wonderful job; Swanage never went short of gas as there were two gasometers, and one was always kept filled.

Station Road in late 1943 with GIs outside the 'Cinema'

56

At Dunesby's I heard or witnessed all the Station Road bombings. On 20th April 1942 two planes machine-gunned the station at 7.15am resulting in Dunesby's roof, along with others, being shot up and the owners, who lived over the shop, forced to move into a bungalow. Shortly after, in another early morning raid an unexploded bomb went through the side wall of Bobby Cann's office, and the army were called out to defuse it. The hole, with the bomb squad trying to defuse it were clearly visible: however we still kept working. On another occasion a Mrs Swaine came into the shop to buy something for her husband's tea. He had a garage at the back of Station Road, where 'Swanage Auto Centre' is now. She said "I must hurry, he'll be home soon". She left the shop about 4.50pm and at 5pm a bomb landed on her house; she was killed, but her baby son was saved. The blast from the bomb blew me through the shop door into the back room.

After just over a year I left Dunesby's and went to work in the 'Cinema' as a projectionist. When the air raid siren sounded during a performance we had to project a slide stating that if anyone wished to leave they could do so, and still return or be issued with a complimentary ticket. Needless to say, no one left and when the 'all clear' sounded we put on another slide to that effect which was always greeted with a loud cheer.

As Swanage had two cinemas the 'Cinema' and the 'Grand', whichever one was showing the best film for three days, had a matinee at 2pm. I had to work in the 'Grand' on Monday afternoons. One day I walked down from my home in Stafford Road at 1.40pm to prepare for work. I could go no further than the corner, where 'Boots' is now, for, as far as the eye could see, Station Road was packed solid with GIs - yes the Yanks had arrived! I tried to push through them, but was told by one "Get in the queue boy!" I tried to tell him that if I didn't find a way through there wouldn't be any show. This changed the situation right away and at the top of his voice he shouted "Make way for the operator". The effect was like the parting of the Red Sea. Unfortunately at this time the 'Grand' had only 414 seats, so there were quite a few disappointed GIs. The 'Cinema' opened at 4.45pm, and once again Station Road was packed. The 'Cinema' had only 141 seats more, so once again there were many disgruntled Americans. However the next day, Bill Maidment the manager, seeing the demand, ordered both cinemas to open at 2pm. However long queues still formed at both cinemas, even after the feature had started for the last showing. The whole programme lasted about three hours, and included a second feature, the main film and the newsreel.

The big difference between the 'Tommies' and the 'Yanks' in their use of the cinema was the amount of rubbish that was left behind after the shows. Every night after the last showing we had to check every row and seat for burning cigarette ends. With the 'Yanks' we'd find packets of cigarettes, sweets and money, so we were always kept well supplied! Whereas the 'Tommies' couldn't afford to leave anything except rubbish!

The 'Cinema' before the war - April 1930

My greatest thrill was showing 'Gone with the Wind' for a week on my own. I was only sixteen at the time and one was supposed to be twenty one to take charge of an operating box. However the other staff were ill, and the two others were working in the 'Cinema'.

Grace's Cafe was opposite the 'Cinema' where 'The Barking Frog' is now and was the busiest cafe in town especially with so many GIs around. It was run by Grace Lefever, her sister and brother in law, Bill. The cook was Mrs Sarah Smith who always walked round barefoot. Lunches were served between 12 noon and 2pm and from 4pm, sausage and chips, egg and chips or just about anything with chips were on the menu. During the war one projectionist would show one reel and have the next one off, so during the evening we used to go across to the cafe for a cup of tea and a chip sandwich. We always had to sit in the kitchen because the cafe was so full. It was so busy that Grace asked me if I could do her books every night when I finished at the 'Cinema'. After she locked up and as it was so dark, I used to walk her back to Cornwall Road where she lived, and then continued on to Stafford Road where we now all lived.

Just before the war ended I was called up and served in the Royal Engineers from 1945-48. Once demobbed I returned to work at the 'Cinema'. The cinemas were owned then by Portsmouth Town Cinemas, but in 1953 they were sold to Tony Whitehouse. The 'Cinema' was then completely revamped with new seating, a larger screen, curtains and concealed lighting, and renamed 'The Ritz'. I remained the only projectionist there until it closed in October 1959.

Brian Street

Brian lived with his family at the Grosvenor during the war. He was six when war broke out and recounts his memories of the hotel and wartime Swanage.

In 1938 my father Fred Street took the position of Secretary to the Exton Group of Hotels, a group of five, two of which were the Grosvenor and the Royal Victoria. Our family took permanent residence at the Grosvenor that October, and in the following summer took the ground floor flat in Rockleigh, one of the two annexes in the hotel grounds which were used as additional guest bedrooms during the summer. It was at Rockleigh that I, then aged six, recall the radio broadcasting the lead up to the outbreak of war, with the hotel gardener Mr Steele routinely listening in through the open window.

Fred Street by Grosvenor pool in 1941

The management at the hotel during the war consisted of the manager Captain Clifford Balls, a member of the Exton family, my father; Barbara Love, the excellent and renowned hostess, Barbara Spence, the most erudite receptionist, and Mr Pledger, the long suffering chef. The Grosvenor clientele at that time comprised, traditional holidaying guests, a few permanent residents, visiting Government officials and serving officers, notably in the early years, those visiting TRE for the regular series of meetings with the scientists known as the Sunday Soviets.

Early in the war the Royal Victoria was taken over for troop billeting along with the annex Rockleigh. The 'Piggeries' at the back of the Royal Victoria was retained. They were tended by a local handicapped man known affectionately as Dummy. He communicated by gesticulation which was more than adequate to make himself understood, as he suffered from both deafness and dumbness. The golf course, now the Prince Albert Gardens, which was also part of the Group and owned by Mrs Balls was given over to sheep grazing.

The bars associated with the hotels were left under the control of the Exton group. Johnnie Stockley a local young man was taken on by my father as barman at the Shades bar in the Royal Victoria, now the East Bar. It became acknowledged that Johnnie's bar was the only bar in town not to have any serious drunken behaviour. Johnnie in an unassuming manner took total control of the customers, predominantly the forces, and became widely respected. He became part of the Grosvenor management team for wartime duties such as firewatching. Many cards from the front in Europe were addressed to 'Johnnie Swanage'.

Once Rockleigh was used as a billet we moved again into the Grosvenor and remained in the main building throughout the war. Of the three ground floor rooms overlooking the swimming pool, two were used as my father's office and our living room, the third was equipped and maintained permanently as a meeting room. This was used for the many conferences held at the Grosvenor. These rooms were later turned into the 'Kidiba'.

My parents came to know Robert Watson-Watt who was the father of radar. He stayed at the hotel when visiting Mr A.P. Rowe, head of TRE. Those staying at the Grosvenor over night on 17th April 1944 before witnessing the Studland rehearsal for D-Day vary from account to account. The list appears to be, The King, Churchill, Eisenhower, Montgomery, General Miles Dempsey and Field Marshal Alan Brooke. Obviously secrecy had been called for relating to these dignitaries staying, as in the war days secrecy and silence were respected. 'Careless talk costs lives' was the then current and pertinent slogan.

Guests using the pool in 1941 with beach defences behind on Buck Shore

Soon after Dunkirk a succession of regiments led by the Grenadier Guards were billeted in Swanage. The Royal Victoria Hotel was used for the South Wales Borderers and later, the American 1st Division in the build up to D-Day. A memory I have was of a fire in the Royal Victoria, smoke was billowing out of one of the windows, when an adjacent window was thrown open, and to the amusement of the onlookers a part shaven GI enquired with immaculate American phraseology "What the hell's going on?"

They were all very friendly especially to youngsters like myself.

My involvement with the raids on Swanage was limited largely to observations after the attack. In the early part of the war bombers passed over Swanage on daylight raids to inland targets, such as the Bristol docks. Air raid sirens were sounded in advance, this was not the case during the later 'tip and run' raids by fighter/bombers. Before Morrison Shelters were issued the Grosvenor guests routinely took shelter in the ballroom. The area on the Downs side was tucked under the hill and therefore offered some protection. The first raid I recall occurred was when on one occasion we were crossing the ballroom to the shelter area, and a bomb was clearly heard passing over the hotel. It fell on the Downs alongside the current car park off Broad Road. This was a night bomber returning from an inland target and jettisoning an unused bomb, presumably with the Pier or the Grosvenor as likely targets.

The indentation is still there, just, with a lone tree growing out of what was once the crater. We visited the site when it became light and I can remember the shrapnel being initially too hot to pick up; we took some, as collecting was already a recognised pastime.

On another occasion when I came out of school at Hill Crest up at Durlston, I decided to delay my walk back home across the Downs to the Grosvenor to watch some Grenadier Guards drilling on the area alongside Bon Accord and Peveril Roads'. While this diversion was happening a 'tip and run' raid came in and dropped bombs nearby, possibly the raid on Park Road in July 1942. On returning I was met on the Downs by a thoroughly distraught and worried mother.

My mother and I witnessed what turned out to be the worst raid of the war later in August when the Westminster Bank received a direct hit. We were on Buck Shore and my mother spotted the plane cross the bay at sea level, climb over Ballard Down, level out, strafe the main beach before dropping its bombs. Buck Shore cleared quickly, and I recall sheltering in the gap between the base of the Grosvenor wall and the pool pump at the back of the beach. In the event the attack did not sweep round the bay to Buck Shore. After the raid which killed eight people and seriously injured eleven others, we visited the site and my memory is of intact jars on a shelf on the wall of a once upper room; an early lesson on the vagaries of bomb blasts.

Later, on a Sunday lunchtime, we heard the bombs which destroyed the Swanage Dairies in The Square. We walked down from the Grosvenor, and I remember the approach to the site covered with cardboard milk bottle tops.

These memories of wartime at the Grosvenor are of a six year old fully occupied with his own life, and very scant, though specific instances remain clear. Hopefully one day research will be able to amplify the day to day operation of the hotel in those turbulent times.

Swanage Dairies in The Square after it was bombed, 23rd August 1942

Nancy Greene

Nancy spent the whole of the war years in Swanage as a schoolgirl, firstly at Mount Scar for two years and subsequently the Grammar School. She lived with her mother Amy, older sister Mary and brother David while her father remained in India.

The war started when I was nine and finished around my sixteenth birthday. It was certainly a very hard and testing time for my mother, as it was for all women on their own.

A large part of the war years we spent at the 'Rookery', a large detached house on what is now described as the Pier Head site adjacent to what was then the Royal Victoria Hotel. Our family were tenants there in the middle flat. In the flat below there were a Miss Weller and Ralph Weller and above a variety of people. Our landlord was the Grosvenor Hotel and our rent was £4 11s 0d a month; I remember this because my mother would give the money to me in an envelope and I would take it to the hotel, go up to the reception and say 'this is the rent for the Rookery'.

There was quite a bit happening on the Rookery triangle . The Pier Head Restaurant, built in 1939, was the Officers Mess for the Royal Welsh Fusiliers. They had a ceremonial goat which they paraded around the place. For some reason they used to come from the Officers Mess each week to borrow my mum's jam tart tins; I don't quite know why they wanted to make jam tarts, but they used to come and borrow everything she had, and return them at the end of the day full of jam tarts!

Opposite us, over the other side of the road, was a grassy area which was used to graze sheep, and in the corner pigs, this is now a small car park and part of Prince Albert Gardens. The area behind the Victoria Hotel was, at one time, pigsties, and at the beginning of the day the pigs were brought over the road to spend the day in the corner of the field.

Air raid warnings regularly sounded from the top of the Town Hall. German planes would fly over the town from France on their way to bomb the Bristol docks. We lay in bed at night listening to the planes coming over and then an hour or so later we would hear the droning sound again, this time coming from the north, as the planes returned to their base. Sometimes the noise of the planes was more confused, as if there were chases or fights going on above us. Each time the siren on the top of the Town Hall would sound and wake us up, and we were thankful once more that we were safe.

After the sun set each day we had the matter of the blackout. No light was permitted outside the house, so there were no street lights. If there was no moon, or if the sky was very overcast, everything was buried in complete darkness. Torches were not really permitted, but people used them briefly when negotiating steps or difficult bits of the road; you just hoped the Air Raid Warden was not patrolling nearby for he might tell you off or, even worse, fine you for endangering the lives of your fellow citizens. All of this meant, of course, that evening activities of every sort were curtailed.

All the windows in every house and building where a light might be expected had to be blacked out by some means. That meant putting up one or two layers of heavy curtains, or obtaining frames covered in black material to fit each window. Traffic requiring headlights was not really permissible at night.

At the Grammar School we had a lot of air raid warnings and you didn't just ignore them. At first there were trenches dug in Day's Park for the school. Now can you imagine, trenches in Day's Park! Well we had to troop out of the school and sit in these trenches. I can't quite remember what we did, Mary's comments were 'you needed wellington boots at least'! Well this didn't last too long because a couple of bombs were dropped in Day's Park, so they thought, well maybe trenches were not such a good idea after all, so when the air raid warnings went off the girls had to go into the cupboard under the stairs. I don't know how we all got in, especially since there were about eighty of us, we sort of sat on top of one another. The boys went into a cupboard at the other end of the school, there were about ninety of them. The prefects were allowed to sit in the cloakroom. Mary also said that in the woodwork room on the ground floor there was a trap door where materials were stored and some children were put down there.

One year we had evacuees at school from Vauxhall in London, the town didn't like them at all. They had school in the afternoon and us in the morning, we were fed up with this, we felt why should we give up our school to them, so we didn't go to school in the afternoon. They also brought their own staff; it was so unsatisfactory it only lasted about six weeks.

The school day started at 9.10am and lasted to 4.10pm and we had compulsory games on Saturday. To start off with, Mary and I went home for lunch at 12 noon and came back at 1.30pm, but later school lunches were introduced and very good they were too. If a number of children attended from the same family the oldest paid 6d the second 5d and the third 4d, wartime coupons were not involved. In the summer the dinner ladies asked us to collect blackberries and they would pay us $1^1/_2$d per lb; they would then give them to us for lunch, either in a pie or on their own.

School meals helped to eke out the rations. I was always hungry at the lunch break because I spent my free time running up and down the rough field chasing a hockey ball. This did help to warm me up; normally there was a minimum amount of heating on in school and, since I always wore little white ankle socks, my legs were always frozen. Jam tart was one of my favourite puddings especially when the tart was filled with a specially sharp, concentrated orange jelly.

We had far more female teachers at school due to the call up. Two men remained, due to their age, Mr Turner and Mr Sellick. The school was quite small with about 180 on roll. Mrs Harvell, she was excellent and came back after retirement to teach maths, but there was a weakness on the science side due to the lack of male teachers. There was an amazing assortment of teachers in wartime. Mr Booker was from some sort of public school. He never had his trousers hitched up properly and had to use a tie! He didn't fit in at all well and kept saying how hopeless everything was; he taught English and didn't last too long.

The other disaster area was art, we had a series of extraordinary women - one woman was quite unbalanced and would talk about anything. We didn't learn a thing. Mary was taking art as her main subject and she failed, which was ridiculous because she went on to Goldsmith's College and did a third year special art. In the end they cancelled art and when I did school certificate the subject was dropped, but later the school got special permission for us to take the School Certificate Art exam.

We were quite used to aircraft coming over the town. We enjoyed watching the dog-fights with the Spitfires darting in and out. Occasionally a plane would be shot down. I remember a German plane being shot down over Ballard Down and everyone got excited and rushed up there. We were told, if there is any sign of danger throw yourself on the ground. This happened to Mary and myself at the far end of Northbrook Road. A fighter/bomber came down the road firing as it went, we flung ourselves on the grass verge and Mary fell on something sharp - she walked home with blood on her leg, and for ever after called it her war wound!

Mary joined the Girls' Training Corps at school run by Miss Sheffield and one evening they held a concert at the Mowlem Institute to raise money; I don't know if she was performing or in the audience. My mother was not keen to let her go - she knew there were lots of lovely young Americans around the town out to pick up a few girlfriends. One of them was Frank, who walked my 15 year old sister home after the performance. We called him 'Frank the Yank'. My mother was very angry and this resulted in a bad time for my sister; but they just wanted to be friendly, nothing more than that.

We had a friend at Newton Grange called Meg Hawes and I would go and visit her. They would always have Americans round there, two or three for lunch or tea, they enjoyed their company very much.

Shopping was done with ration books: each week 2oz fat, 8oz sugar, 2s (10p) meat, 1lb of jam or marmalade each month, and so on. We never saw a banana. We knew that many ships bringing in food supplies were sunk by German U-boats. The daily paper consisted of one folded sheet. It was many years in our house before we had a radio. There were no televisions. We carried our gas mask box everywhere.

Boys' shoes needed fewer coupons, so I wore boys' shoes. When we grew out of our clothes we sometimes passed them on to other families. It was not necessarily that they could not afford to buy new things, but most likely they were not available in the shops. Quite early on my mother taught us to darn our socks until there seemed more darn than sock, and to wear clothes full of patches was no disgrace.

Food ration books were issued to everyone in January 1940. Rations varied throughout the war according to supply and in the post-war period, rations for some goods were cut even further (e.g. bread was rationed for the first time in July 1946). Meat was the last product to be de-rationed, in July 1954.

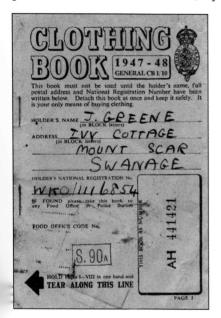

Each man, woman and child had 66 coupons a year

Mary and I both had a weekly allowance of one shilling and with this we had to buy a National Savings stamp at school on Monday mornings and that cost six old pence, half of our weekly income. Then a penny was earmarked for church collection and the remaining five pence was to cover all other expenses: gifts for the family and friends on their birthdays and at Christmas, paint if we needed it for our art lessons, rubbers and pens and crayons and other items for our school work.

I sometimes wondered how I could supplement my income. The only thing which I came up with was to grow geraniums. I could buy a geranium for six old pence, complete with a pot. If I took cuttings and was able to grow more plants, I could then sell these for six pence. The main trouble was that I needed a start-up sum of money to buy the original plant and the pots which I would need later. Also I knew I was not very good at marketing: whom could I approach to buy a geranium plant? The scheme never took off. Not many people seemed to be interested at that time in buying geraniums anyway!

The war ended around my sixteenth birthday with victory in the Far East. My father was in India throughout the war, this long separation was certainly not what my parents had planned. Victory in war always comes with a heavy price, and someone has to pay.

The view looking across Institute Road towards the Parade after the Westminster Bank, Bruton's the ironmongers and Espley's the chemist were destroyed in the bombing on 17th August 1942.

Margaret Hughes

Margaret worked as a shorthand typist during the war. She came down to Swanage from Dundee in April 1940 to work in the radar establishment.

Margaret in 1941

I worked at the radar establishment in Dundee as a shorthand typist with two friends Betty Hillen and Pauline Pretty. In fact we had all started at Bawdsey during 1939 when war was declared. Pauline and I travelled up by road from there to Dundee and we heard Mr Chamberlain's declaration on the Sunday when we were in a car, by the side of the road, on the England/Scotland border. Betty and I were seventeen and Pauline was nineteen. Mr A.P. Rowe, the Superintendent of the Establishment called everyone together during our stay in Dundee and said that a place was being built for us at Swanage and that it would be 'A quiet little backwater for the duration'.

The whole group of two hundred people were moved to Swanage in April 1940. I travelled by train with Betty and Pauline from Dundee to London and thence to Swanage. When we arrived at Corfe Castle it was such a surprise with wonderful views from the train, so unexpected, as I'd never heard of Corfe Castle. When we arrived in Swanage one of the first things we did was walk down to the sea. Betty said to me later in life "After working in Felixstowe and Dundee I fell in love with the place, as I'd never seen anything so beautiful".

We obtained digs in Locarno Road run by Nancy and Sidney Smith; Mrs Smith was a wonderful cook, such good company, and the place was a real home from home. Betty and Pauline stayed for the whole two years with them, but I went to live with my family who had also moved down to Swanage: this was due to the fact that my father also worked in the Establishment as an administration officer. None of us knew exactly what to expect after our arrival, but Betty remembers, 'The first air raid warning of the war, and firemen running down King's Road to the fire station, frantically trying to fix on their gas masks'.

Things became quite crowded at Worth and after Dunkirk in June 1940 things warmed up, for we had a number of air raid warnings. Before the shelters were built we all had to go down into the valley; I sprained my ankle but Mrs Smith put a cold bandage on it and I survived! When the shelters were constructed they were underground, and could each hold about forty people. I became quite good at darts! There was one occasion in 1942 when the staff were in the canteen for lunch and didn't have time to reach the shelter before bombs were dropped nearby. People shouted to get under the tables, but they were quite small so there were a number of heads and shoulders taking shelter with many bottoms sticking out:- it must have been quite a sight. However there were casualties and, I think, fatalities on the R.A.F. site a few fields away. Leeson had been taken over earlier as was Durnford and Forres, so the groups were well spread around.

I used to work on each of the sites. When I moved to Leeson after Dunkirk I had an office on my own looking out towards the Isle of Wight and I remember wondering, 'Will they come today'.

It was a beautiful day and ideal for anything to happen. I never thought we would lose the war and I don't really think many people did. Another sight I remember at that time was the starlit sky. There were no street lights because of the blackout and the stars were very closely packed together. I have never seen the night skies so beautiful since.

Robert Watson-Watt, A.P. Rowe and the Duke of Kent visiting Durnford House in 1941

I worked as a Shorthand Typist Grade 1, as did Betty and Pauline, but they stayed on the Worth site the whole time, working in the typing pool. We were picked up for work in a bus around 8.30am and started at 9am. We finished at 5.30pm but sometimes stayed later, catching a later bus back to Swanage with the workshop staff who worked longer hours. There were guards at the Worth site who saw us in and out, and we had to present our passes. We worked mostly three or four to a room and were attached to a group. When the Establishment was expanded more typing staff were taken on and distributed around the sites, so their numbers increased to five or six at each site. When we finished on one job we would go over and pick up reports and letters that were in the tray waiting to be typed, most of which were very technical and secret.

Everything that we typed was checked by two people working together as proof readers, one to read the original material and the other to check the typescript. All the typewriters were manual. If copies were required (and there were no such things as photocopiers in those days) they had to be banged out on the typewriter, with a carbon between each sheet. One tried to make sure there were no mistakes because if there were each copy would have to be corrected with a rubber which we called a 'Charlie'. If quite a number of copies were required a stencil was typed; this was then placed on a hand-operated Gestetner duplicating machine to run off the copies. If we made mistakes when we typed a stencil we used correcting fluid. It was all very interesting and very mathematical at times; I for one never really understood what it all meant, but there was never a boring moment. Because of the nature of the work most of the correspondence that went out had to be put in a plain envelope marked 'Secret', and then put in a registered envelope.

All the post was handled in the Registry. This was a glorified post room but also kept secret files and records. Special messengers went from there to deliver correspondence to other buildings and sites. One aspect of our work was taking dictation from the Technical Officer who went through the post every day and making a précis of everything scientific that might be of interest to the senior staff. The typing consisted of a top copy plus eleven or twelve carbon copies on special cigarette type paper.

We worked five and a half days a week which included Saturday morning up until noon, this was quite standard in this country at the time. We were probably paid between £2 and £2.10s a week but this included an accommodation allowance. We received an extra 5/- a week for passing an RSA exam in typing and 3/- for shorthand. This extra amount was because we had already passed these standards and taken an exam at work. If we obtained a pay rise it was normally about 3/- a week. Equal pay didn't come in until after the war, and until women were called up they had to leave work when they married. Every woman over a certain age had to report to the employment exchange and they would then assess whether you had to be sent away on war related work. Later on at the Establishment we all worked on a Sunday, and Saturday was our full day off. This was because of the Superintendent's

'Sunday Soviets'. Sunday was considered an important day because it was the only time some of the high ranking officers could attend meetings, so we had to work, and earned a bit of overtime.

Our breaks at work consisted of an hour for lunch. Sometimes, those working at Worth would go up to the Square and Compass pub or walk down towards Chapmans Pool. We had a short break in the mornings and afternoons and would occasionally go up to a wooden tea hut run by the James family from Renscombe Farm, but usually we brewed our own tea.

Having all day Saturday free gave us more time to go shopping in Bournemouth. The buses were more frequent then and the return fare was about 2/6d. Sometimes I went to an Ice Cream Parlour in Station Road opposite the cinemas. There I would have a cup of coffee with a big blob of cream on top, this costing about one shilling. Leisure time activities, other than shopping in Bournemouth, were walking, often over the hills to Corfe and catching the train back, going to the cinema, or staying at home in the evenings reading, knitting or doing a little gardening. By this time I was living with my family so did not always join in the walks.

Most people were in the Air Raid Precautions and were required to go out when the alarms sounded: this I did not like much. There was one raid on the 20th April 1942 when the early train was due to leave the station at 7.15am. Montague Purchase, the grocery shop on the corner of Station Road, next to the Post Office took a direct hit and the train was machine gunned.

After a surprise raid on the German radar establishment at Bruneval it was thought that there would be reprisals. As a consequence, after each day all the papers would have to be taken to the Registry each evening and be locked up. This room was made ready to be blown up if necessary and soldiers were put on guard outside as it contained so much secret material. Things happened very quickly for us; Betty was in the cinema one evening and was called to the office where she was told to report to Malvern the next day. Transport was provided for the rest of us a little later and we all set off, each with a small suitcase. We typists were lucky, as we did not have to look for digs but were given rooms in what had earlier been the boys' dormitories in Malvern College. We never saw Swanage again until after the war.

Houses in The Narrows destroyed as a result of the bombing raid on 17th August 1942

Tony Meates

Tony was eleven when the war broke out and had just started at the Grammar School. In his spare time he worked as a paper boy and during these duties was wounded in a 'hit & run' raid. Later in April 1943 he joined the Army as an apprentice fitter.

I had just left St. Joseph's Catholic School in Chapel Lane and was due to start at the Grammar School when the war broke out.

The early days of the war saw 1400 evacuees and their teachers descend on Swanage, these children had to be accommodated and taught in the Swanage schools. The Grammar School was disrupted and as a result of having extra children to cope with we had to change the school times to that of a shift system. Mornings one week and afternoons the following week, plus Saturday mornings.

Tony as a Sea Cadet in 1941

At school I can remember that part of the playing fields behind the caretaker's house were dug and planted with vegetables, and these were available to the children and their families.

At that time I was living at Melbury a guest house in Cranborne Road, with my mother, sister Wendy and younger brother Terry. My older brother Desmond had just joined the RAF as an Apprentice Aircraft Electrician. My mother had bought the house in Cranborne Road in 1933 after my father died. It had ten bedrooms and her idea was to turn it into a guest house in order to provide for her four children, this she did on her own.

At the age of twelve in 1940 I got myself a job as a paper delivery boy in Mr. Rose's newsagent shop in Station Road, where Ashley's is now. My morning delivery round was to houses in Cranborne Road, Ilminster Road, and Victoria Avenue. I used, with two other boys, to meet the early morning train at about 6.45am to collect the papers and take them to the shop for sorting into the various rounds. Each boy sorted his own papers for subsequent delivery to the allocated houses on their round. Woe betide any boy who forgot to sort and deliver the correct paper to each house.

I used to use my mother's bike because she had a basket fitted to the handlebars' in which I put most of the papers that were to be delivered to the houses towards the end of the round. The papers at the start of the round were carried in a canvas bag supplied by Mr. Rose.

At about this time I also got myself enrolled as a messenger with the local Air Raid Precautions service. My job was to carry messages between the various ARP posts in and around Swanage. This job I could only do when I was not at school.

Swanage soon became the target, along with virtually every other coastal town, of the Luffwaffe's 'hit & run' raids by fighter bombers. When there was a raid on and the air raid siren was sounding, all of us at school would have to leave our classrooms and be escorted by teaching staff to slit trenches that had been dig across Day's Park. The trenches were about five or six feet deep so we were well protected from any danger should the need arise - it never did!

One day I shall never forget was 20th April 1942, this was Hitler's birthday. It was about 7.15am, the paper boys had just finished sorting the papers in the back room and had started to go outside to start the delivery rounds. I was just putting the papers in the basket on the bike when I heard the sound of planes coming over the railway station. This was followed by the rattle of machine gun fire. I jumped into the nearest doorway, now the entrance to Neville-Jones Solicitors' office. There followed a large thud as a bomb hit the road around where the mini roundabout is now. The bomb bounced on the road and landed on the second floor of what used to be Thresher's Off Licence. I crouched, huddled up against the door. There was a very loud explosion and everything went black with clouds of smoke, dirt and flying debris from the building opposite. The next thing I knew was feeling blood running down my cheek from my right ear and face and a sharp pain in my right leg.

Everything happened so quickly and then everything went quiet and gradually the dust and debris settled. I came out of the doorway just as Fred Jackman came out of the paper shop. He saw I was bleeding and took me down to a First Aid post in a building behind the Trocadero. Sadly I found myself next to several very badly injured soldiers who were at the station at the time of the attack. Others in the vicinity were killed, Cyril and Lily Smith, Arthur Williams and a Royal Navy volunteer Sub.Lt. Bertram Ewers.

I was immediately put on a stretcher and had dressings put on my ear, face and right leg. I was taken up to Swanage Cottage Hospital and there I was attended to by a nurse and put in a bed on one of the wards. I found out afterwards that my injuries were caused by splinters of shrapnel from the exploding bomb. These were removed by a doctor, although one piece was left in behind my ear and was not removed until some months later.

Bearing in mind the incident happened at 7.15am, it was not until after 11am that my mother found out I was in hospital. She had been looking for me amongst the debris surrounding the entrance to the paper shop, and had obviously seen her bike covered in dirt and dust still propped up against the wall, and began to worry where I was. Eventually she found my friend Fred who told her where he had taken me. After enquiries at the First Aid post she came up to the hospital where she was told I'd only suffered minor injuries. I was kept in hospital for three days under observation in case of delayed shock.

I recovered quickly, went back to school and started delivering papers again, this time with Swanage Newspapers just opposite Mr. Rose's badly damaged shop.

At home we were issued with a Morrison table shelter, a large metal table, about six feet by four and about three feet high. All four sides were covered in a removable square mesh designed to stop any debris from entering the shelter. My family either slept in the shelter or under the stairs, apparently the safest place in the event of a direct hit. Luckily we never had to put this to the test.

Trixi Meates

We managed alright as far as food was concerned. We had a large garden and mother used to keep chickens and rabbits, so this, combined with the authorised rations meant we usually had a adequate supply of food for the family. Occasionally we went and had a lunch at the local British Restaurant, which was located in the old part of the United Reformed Church.

In my spare time I, along with my mates, would watch the dog-fights overhead between the RAF's Spitfires and the Luftwaffe's Messerschmitt 109s. If we saw any planes shot down nearby we would get on our bikes and get to the crash site as soon as possible, hoping to pick up any bits and pieces of the crashed aircraft to keep as souvenirs. At the time we thought this to be very exciting. Some crash sites that came to mind were Kingston, Harmans Cross and Studland. I still have a small notebook in which I recorded the name of the German pilot of a 109 that was shot down near Worth Matravers on 9th June 1941. His name was Ober Lt. Werner

Machold. I don't remember what happened to him, I believe he was sent to a POW camp.

Later we, as a family, were forced to move from Melbury our guest house in Cranborne Road as it was requisitioned for use by the WAAFs in the later part of 1943. We went to live in an old bungalow in Newton Road until the end of the war when we were able to return.

In April 1943 when I was fifteen I persuaded my mother to let me join the army as an apprentice, which she agreed to, probably because I'd be away from the raids on Swanage. The Army Apprentice School was in Chepstow in South Wales. I applied and was asked to attend an examination board in Dorchester to test my fitness and mental agility. Luckily I passed and was accepted as an apprentice fitter, which eventually allowed me to become a fitter in the Royal Engineers.

Six months after I joined the Apprentice School two of my classmates, Fred Jackman and David Warr joined me. So there were three ex Swanage Grammar School boys all being trained there at the same time by the army as future tradesmen and Warrant Officers in the Royal Engineers and Royal Electrical and Mechanical Engineers.

During the time I was at the Army Apprentice School, Dorset became a restricted access area due to the build up of troops for the D-Day landings. This included the American 1st Division based in Swanage. As a result I had to obtain a special pass to allow me to come back to Swanage to visit my family.

While I was on leave in Swanage I met some of the GIs who were billeted in the hotels. One GI called Tex Carter used to visit our house prior to D-Day in 1944. My mother probably got to know him because she used to sing in Betty Tunnell's concert party, which used to go round the area entertaining the troops. As a result of these visits many of the soldiers were invited to visit families in Swanage.

My mother always wondered whether Tex survived the onslaught on Omaha Beach on D-Day. After she died I found some photographs of him in her belongings. I have made enquiries with the American 1st Division in the USA as well as with other GIs who were billeted in Swanage, all without success. I am continuing my search in the hope that someone might know what happened to Tex and whether he survived the D-Day landings.

Tex Carter

Brenda Langdon

After leaving St. Joseph's Convent School Brenda went to work in the office at Barratt's Garage. Before the war Brenda learnt to dance, and during the war years was part of Betty Tunnell's dance troupe that went around the area entertaining the troops.

I was brought up at 327 High Street and there were six of us in the family, three boys and three girls. When I left the Convent School at fourteen I went straight into work at Barratt's Garage and was paid 10/- a week. The garage was located on the site of the present Post Office in King's Road. I started working in the office, dealing with the accounts and stores.

The workshop was run by Cyril Farr, who was a first class mechanic and many young lads served their apprenticeships in the workshop under him. To keep me out of the forces or war work I had to complete a set amount of hours in the workshop. I quite enjoyed the work and the lads taught me about cylinder head gaskets and how to grind the valves etc. Although petrol coupons were in operation in the war years there were many cars driving around to repair and service as well as the trades using lorries, such as The Alderney Dairy around the corner. The military took over the garage and we moved to 164 High Street where Jewsons is now.

When I was young I longed to learn to dance, so I asked my mother and she said "Oh I don't know". It cost a shilling a lesson and we were not well off. Anyway I started at the age of ten, and was taught by Betty Tunnell at her hall which was located in the High Street where Arkwrights is now.

Betty Tunnell was well loved in Swanage and a local personality. After training as a dancer she spent some years dancing professionally, but then came back to Swanage and decided to start a dancing school. She also began a long run of Swanage pantomimes which started before the war. When the war broke out these shows were put on hold, but Betty formed a Concert Party by keeping some dancers and members, including her husband Bern. Before she was called away to do war work in other parts of the country the Concert Party ran shows for the troops around the area.

Betty Tunnell

I was selected as one of the dancers for the Troupe. Betty was a very persuasive person so if she decided you were going to take part it happened! My mother was worried because we went all over the area entertaining, such as Arne - she considered it dangerous and was worried for my safety.

The Concert Party was made up of about ten or twelve of us. It was a mixed performance - dancing, singing, tap dancing, piano playing, comedy and sometimes a ventriloquist. Betty's husband Bern was a very talented entertainer, having started as a clog dancer in the halls, in a troupe called 'The Eight Lancashire Lads'. One of the lads in this troupe was Charlie Chaplin; later he left and went off to the States to make his fortune. Bern, as well as being a tap dancer, could play the piano; in fact he could tap dance and play the piano simultaneously, which took some doing. He also had a rich bass voice and could do a turn as a ventriloquist. He was a valued member of the Concert Party.

The Concert Party dancers
From left: Brenda Langdon, Mary Bonfield, Margarita Bonfield, Joy Smith

We entertained the troops in many billets in Swanage - the Royal Victoria Hotel, Craigside Hotel and Forres School - as well as the Knoll House Hotel, Bovington, Arne, and even Brownsea Island.

The show was like a variety concert. It started with the five of us girls dancing in a row, then you would have someone singing, then probably a comedy act, which was Bern, then Betty would do a turn to get them going. We never received any payment, we just loved performing. Sometimes the changing room facilities were very uncomfortable or strange, such as the crypt of Kingston church or a paint shed!

The GIs must have liked our troupe of dancers because three of the girls ended up marrying Americans - Joy, Margarita and her sister Mary. They started off as friendships because, like in our family, the GIs came round to our houses. I can remember them using our stove to cook their popcorn!

One evening several of us were invited to the York House Hotel by the Americans. We had an amazing meal. At home, cooking was very standard and our food was limited due to rationing. But there, nothing was spared, it was wonderful.

I also worked, with several friends, as a voluntary waitress some evenings at the Service Canteen and Rest Area at the Trocadero in The Square. It could be used by anyone in the forces, British or American. It served basic fare - Welsh rarebit, beans or spaghetti on toast, rock cakes etc. The canteen was very popular and well patronised.

My friend Pat Tunnell was also occasionally in the Concert Party as a child performer. She takes up the story from here.

Betty Tunnell was my aunt and I was brought up in a large guest house in Cranborne Road. I lived there with my grandmother and grandfather who was a local tailor, my mother Phyl, Betty and her husband Bern Hardy. During the war it was extremely busy, a bit like living in Waterloo station!

Part of The Concert Party
Back row: Freda Pond, Unknown, Betty, Mr Callum, Paddy Callum
Front: Marg Bonfield, Joy Smith, Elsie Pond, Brenda Langdon, Mary Bonfield

As a child I was occasionally part of the Concert Party. We once did a show for the troops stationed on Brownsea Island. The idea of having me in the party was that the men would be touched to watch this little child dancing, and be reminded of home. I remember nothing of the concert, only the peacocks on the island and their wonderful feathers that I collected and kept for ages.

On another occasion when I was part of the team, I remember walking back from Forres School with my mother in the total darkness of the blackout and suddenly being confronted by a soldier who barked at us, "Halt - who goes there?" I gripped my mother's hand, but I knew she was terrified.

The Concert Party dancers
From left: Margarita, Joy, Elsie, Brenda, Mary

Betty treated everyone the same and when the Americans arrived there was one black GI who took a shine to her, I think it was because he was not treated well by his white counterparts. Betty showed kindness towards him and so he followed her around everywhere, we used to laugh about it, as he said she reminded him of his mother.

Our guest house accommodated all sorts of soldiers who came to stay if they were on leave, and their wives came down to stay with them. Well we did have one lady staying, her name was Rosie, she was English but married to a GI. I remember one day coming in the front door with my grandmother. Upon entering we were confronted by four GIs sitting up the stairs, almost in a queue. So my grandmother said, "Yes can I help you", to which one of them replied, "Oh hi, ma'am, Miss Rosie here is so lonely, her husband's gone off to the war and so we've come round to keep her company". My grandmother remarked, "Sometimes I think I need a red light outside".

Another time I rushed to the front door to find a very smart soldier and a row of tanks parked all along Cranborne Road. He saluted smartly, "Transport reporting for Concert Party ma'am".

Once I met an American army cook whose name was Tex. He used to go round to our neighbours the Meates's who also ran a guest house. Through Tex we were invited to a wonderful party thrown by an American unit in a large house in Newton Road. It was the first time I'd ever tasted angel cake, yum, yum.

I remember when the American troops were leaving Swanage they sent batches of ring donuts round to the schools, one for each child, as a thank you to the town.

Brenda's sister Kathleen, with wartime beach defences behind

Bill Squibb

Bill was brought up in a house in Taunton Road, and was five when war broke out. His playground was Durlston and he knew the area like the back of his hand, observing the comings and going of the troops in the area.

Our family lived at the top of Taunton Road, about 100 yards below the water tower, in a house that looked right along Queens Road to the hospital. Until late 1941 my father Willis and his brother 'Drew' operated private hire 'posh' cars for M.A. Squibb & Sons (they being 'the sons'). 'Drew' died and not long after my father was called up into the Army, even though he was then a one man business. He was supposedly in a reserved occupation due to the fact that he was a one person business, and therefore the sole provider for the family. However the army manpower was so stretched at that time that the next upper age group was required.

I started at the Infant class at Mount Scar in 1937/8. Once war started the authorities did their best to protect us from blast and shrapnel damage while at school. Windows were taped, like noughts and crosses to prevent shards of broken glass flying around. Windows also had blackout panels of beaded wood and light cloth which were more effective than drawn curtains. Externally all doorways were shielded by sandbag blast barriers ten feet tall. External bomb shelters were located in the playground. These were very thick, solid and curved to deflect missiles of one kind or another, and were partially sunk into the ground to give added protection from a sideways blast.

The authorities didn't do quite so well with respect to digging zig-zag trenches for us over the road at the Queens Mead field. They obviously had the First World War in mind. These trenches filled up with water in no time and were basically useless, as they were far too remote from the school. A 'hit and run' raid would be as good as over, with the aircraft already flying back to France before we had even left the classroom!

The whole town was invaded by 1400 London evacuees in early

September 1939. The situation was initially quite overwhelming. It ended up with us attending school in the mornings only, and the London children attending in the afternoon. We all learnt a new street-wise 'blue' language. I once tried out a word that I had learnt on my father; he was extremely shocked, almost as though an arrow had gone through his heart!

Since I was born and brought up in the Durlston area, in the war it became my playground. Durlston at that time was like a forest to me with trees everywhere. The houses were shaded by huge trees and their boundaries shrouded by tall impenetrable hedges. In most places the trees used to grow over the roads touching one another in the centre and creating tunnels.

In 1940 I was six years old and along with my best friends Bernard Dodd and David Hunt, took in all that I saw. We three became experts at climbing through the thousands of miles of barbed wire, especially the 'swiss roll' type which was expanded to stretch over long distances. We entered at the end and the central tunnel was no barrier to us small boys. In this time of austerity torn clothing was a concern when we returned home, but scratches, were not so bad and soon healed.

Boys war games 'acquired' badges and clothing, and we also became expert on aircraft recognition. We had 20/20 vision in those days. I knew all the army ranks and badges from Private to Field Marshal, as well as those of the Navy and R.A.F. To us, it all seemed most important to know the pecking order and equivalent status of each armed service.

I soon had a real life experience on the 14th May 1941. I was playing with two pals on the downs just off Seymer Road, on what is now the parallel footpath. Four Messerschmitt 109 fighter/bomber aircraft came in low over Durlston Bay, hopped up over the downs and proceeded to machine gun the seafront and bomb the town. It was the first of many 'hit and run' raids on Swanage, and left us kids gaping in wonder. The planes were grey, with the black swastika picked out on a yellow background and a yellow spinner right in front of the nose propeller; the pilots could be clearly seen. For us this was the real thing!

Soldiers were billeted in all the large houses and private hotels in the Durlston area, and as a small boy I visited most of them. The houses were vacated private dwellings which had been left by the owners who wanted to escape the likely south coast front line or private hotels which were redundant in wartime due to the non-existent holiday trade.

The first soldiers to arrive were from the British army and could have been compared to 'Dad's Army'! As I lived nearby I used to watch them in Grosvenor Road and Cluny Crescent. Fixed bayonets, always drill marching, crunch, crunch - turn about 1-2-3-4 crunch, crunch, crunch, with the very unified rhythm of their hobnail boots. Now and again a small group, just down from the water tower, had bren gun drill, strip - assembly - click - ready, time and again. Many regiments came and went, the Grenadier Guards early on, and then the Royal Welsh Fusiliers, who were very good for church parades as they had a regimental goat, with large curved horns that was paraded around regularly.

Then in November 1943 the Americans arrived; this was all entirely new, and I watched them arriving in the Durlston area. They walked up Taunton Road, about thirty or forty soldiers in battledress, to their first billets. They had armfuls of coat hangers, broom sticks and brushes. They were going to live, for a short time, in clean rooms and wear smart 'walking out' uniforms. I was very excited and ran home to tell mum I'd seen my first black man!

I liked having the GIs around and started to chat to them. By this time I was nine years old then and began thinking, 'we can't lose the war, we have a rich and powerful friend, we will definitely win', and so in general life became more positive and less tense. Even as young children we knew very well how the war was going, as we sensed it. When I saw the GIs in the streets their basic diet seemed to be chewing gum in long flat strips, cigars and crush-pack cigarettes - Camel, Lucky Strike, Chesterfield and Philip Morris. Their marching, when they did it, was casual and training had more to do with tossing a baseball around and being able to catch it in their large gloves.

The GIs wore either battledress when training or walking out uniforms which they wore around town when off duty. The walking out uniforms were made of smooth cloth, with olive green tunics, collar and tie, fawn trousers, neat shoes, and a mass of brass buttons, badges and rank displays. The Americans had invented, and used, shirts with buttons down the front, whereas the British still had the night shirt type which was pulled over one's head. One difference in the battledress was with the ankle gaiters, as the GIs had under instep stirrup loops with zig-zag lace hooks up to below the knee, while the British gaiters were very short, used two straps, and made the thick rough trousers look like plus-fours. The American fighting boots were high ankle, lightweight with thick rubber soles, whereas the British boot was of the sturdy hobnail variety made of leather.

Three GIs in 'walking out' uniforms by the Great Globe

We always found the GIs very friendly and they liked us kids. They loved soft covered books, including American comics and were avid readers of Superman, Captain Marvel, Batman, Captain

Midnight, Spiderman and Wonderwoman.

We visited all the GI billets around us especially their food stations! One such food station was the Minterne Hotel in Park Road, and I, plus two other scruffs were invited in and given jam tarts with lattice work pastry attached, naturally, being American, each tart was the size of a carpet tile - we ate the lot! Another time we visited Craig-y-Don, a large house at the top of the downs in Belle Vue Road. Here we were given half filled ten gallon drums of peaches and pears; with scooped hands we polished them off as well. The other delicacy we came across was powdered egg; this was a new experience for us, but it tasted really lovely.

The equipment at Durlston was quite substantial in the build up to D-Day. Queen's Road, Bon Accord Road, Durlston Road, Sunnydale Road and Solent Road all housed American mobile gun carriers. There were always a few soldiers hanging around reading comics etc. but they had no problem with us jumping up to swivel and elevate the guns on the gun carriers. We also started up large troop lorries which had push button starters and didn't require keys. They accepted kids doing this sort of thing but an adult would be a different matter and they wouldn't allow them near their equipment. Jeeps too were everywhere, and they would hop into their Jeeps just to travel one hundred yards. The soldiers would roar off, and when arriving at their destination would drive up on to the curb braking at the last moment. There was no such thing as coasting to save fuel; they simply wanted to check that the machines operated to their maximum efficiency.

They also possessed walkie-talkie wireless sets. I remember watching them on the old Stone Quay, operating from their Jeep which had a large pull-out aerial at the back, talking to one another. They also had morse code sets, and they relayed messages to one another, probably across the water to others in the Ocean Bay area. The morse code operators would have triple writing pads that flipped over to the left and right to take messages in triplicate. They were testing the equipment to check that it all worked correctly.

In the corner of a field where Durlston Road meets Peveril Road the GIs put up scramble cargo netting. At the time there were tall trees there and they fixed a large beam of wood between two trees and straddled it with this netting which was made up of large squares of thick rope. This was used for soldiers to practise scrambling up cliffs, or the sides of ships. However it was just great for us kids, it was almost as though it had been put there for us! We were fearless, and we felt that if we fell off and hit the ground we would bounce! We loved playing on them.

All the small US equipment of one kind or another, came in wooden boxes, such as ammunition boxes and long boxes for guns. These came in half inch wood casings which were olive green in colour. These large boxes stood on their ends like a sentry box and provided garden toolsheds for years after. All these containers would have been destroyed long before if they hadn't been used by us locals.

At the end of the day, at five or six o'clock, three cavalry trumpeters sounded off outside the Durlston Court Hotel. When they heard this all the GIs stood to attention, wherever they were or whichever direction they were facing. This was one of the few displays of mass obedience and confounded their otherwise casual approach.

We kids were sad when they left, for they were kind to us, great fun, and made our lives more colourful than otherwise would have been the case. After they left we fed for weeks on tinned meat and vegetables discarded by the US forces. A short time later, when staying with my uncle at Worth Matravers, I witnessed the red glow over the horizon from Worth pond. This told us that the Allies were now visiting someone else! D-Day had started on the 6th June 1944.

Ivan Lock

Ivan was born and bred in Swanage. During the war he worked as a telephone engineer for two years doing installation work at secret locations. When he was twenty years old he was called up into the Royal Navy and worked as an electrical artificer on warships.

When I was young I lived above the Co-op store in the High Street, where my father was the manager. There were five of us in our family: I had two older sisters. When I left Mount Scar School at the age of fourteen I went to work as a telegraph boy at Swanage Post Office.

Soon after the war began I was given the opportunity to transfer to Bournemouth as an apprentice engineer. The training scheme was very intensive, covering all aspects of telecommunications. My wages of 23 shillings a week unfortunately did not cover my lodging costs in Bournemouth, so I asked if I could continue my training in the Swanage area, then I could live at home. I was told that this could be arranged, provided I agreed to continue my engineering studies at Bournemouth Technical College.

I attended college three nights a week from 7-9.30pm throughout the year. In those days there was no such thing as day release or time off in lieu. With the change having been agreed, I travelled from Swanage to college by bicycle, and at the end of each session I did voluntary all-night firewatching at various Post Office buildings in Bournemouth. Each building usually had two people firewatching. There would be a couple of beds for us to sleep on, but if the air raid siren sounded we had to rush up to the roof with our tin hats and fire fighting equipment. Most nights I was not disturbed and was able to sleep right through. However there were occasions when I had no sleep, or at best broken sleep; this was not helpful because at daybreak I had to cycle back to Swanage via the ferry and start a normal day's work at 8am. There were no excuses, one had to be there on time or else!

During the war the ferry was used in the normal way, it was only a very small craft. Swanage was a protected area during wartime so, if you came home on the bus from Bournemouth, a soldier would board it at Sandbanks and check your passes; if you didn't have the right documentation you were turfed off. However, those who lived in Swanage were issued with a special document which enabled them to travel to and fro. The return fare to Bournemouth was about 2/6d, and if I went over as a foot passenger it was 3d and with my bike as well, around 9d.

At the age of eighteen I qualified as an installation technician, and as I lived in Swanage many jobs within the area were allocated to me. When I installed pieces of equipment at various secret locations, I was sometimes aware what they were to be used for, and sometimes not. One of my first jobs, which was in Spring 1941, was in a single underground bunker at the top of the Downs in Swanage. I was told to go there, the components were delivered and I fitted a switchboard. At that time the bunker was not being used, as it was still being set up, so I never saw any military personnel at all. The reinforced concrete structure was about 15ft from the cliff edge, with the concrete roof turfed over at ground level. Concrete steps led down to the bunker which consisted of a small room for the switchboard and office work along with a toilet. The switchboard I installed was floor-standing and had 5 lines which were connected underground to Swanage Telephone Exchange. There were also facilities for up to 20 extensions. I could not think where these extensions went, but in wartime no questions were asked.

The bunker was highly secret and was used originally as a Coastal Defence radar site. CD radar operated in combination with coastal gun batteries and was therefore the responsibility of the army. They were used to improve anti-aircraft gun direction and also to track ships to aid coastal defence. The radar installations were mounted on turntables and were turned to point towards a target, giving accurate bearing and range. Many Coast Defence sites around the shore, including the one at Swanage, were staffed by the WRNS (Womens Royal Naval Service), and since the radar site was close to TRE at Worth it was serviced by radar mechanics from there. However in 1942 the site was taken over by an undercover RAF detachment known as 'J Watch'. They occupied the Downs site from the time when planning for the D-Day invasion commenced, two years before the event. The gantry then sprouted all shapes and sizes of radio aerials as J Watch's task was to search the airwaves for enemy communications to assist the code breakers at Bletchley Park.

Although now the entrance is covered over with a concrete slab, the extent of the concrete roof area with turf on top can still be seen.

Another location with which I was concerned was off the Kingston to Chapman's Pool Road. The site was in a large field past a wooded area on the right called the Plantation. This too was highly secret and was one of a network of 'Y Service' listening stations. I once visited the location with a maintenance engineer from the Swanage Telephone Exchange, and remember there were two or three huts used as living accommodation along with two mobile trailer vans containing radio receiving equipment. These were staffed out by Czech or Polish WAAF girls who spoke perfect German. The 'Y Service' was the principal vehicle for listening to and intercepting of enemy communications. They also monitored the radio telephony transmissions of the German forces in the field and in the air. Prior to this CH radar was installed in the field as a stand-by in case the TRE at Worth was put out of action. Later the equipment was moved to Hengistbury Head.

The Radar site at Kingston under construction 1940

Aerial view of Radar site at Kingston 1940

In late 1941 I worked at Lytchett Manor, which was run by the Army. All the anti-aircraft guns in the area were controlled from the Gun Operations Room at Lady Lees Manor, Lytchett Minster. From this Gun Operations Room they controlled the Wareham area, Brownsea Island and through to Swanage. Every anti-aircraft gun site was connected back to them via GPO cables. Some of the sites such as Arne, were in remote locations. At the Manor my job was to pick up the circuits that came in underground and extend them through to the switchboard. The main switchboard was in the hall surrounded by an upstairs balcony. There was a number of girls operating there in teams of about six, and working shifts round the clock; I believe they were called gun plotters.

In connection with my work at The Manor one of the tasks was to run a cable to the anti-aircraft site at Arne; this was located on heathland to the right before Arne village proper. It was inaccessible, off the road, and away from the Post Office lines, which were overhead telephone wires on the Arne Road that came from Stoborough. I had an unenviable job because I had to pick up the GPO wires and extend them down to the gun using Army material called Don 8. The wire was very difficult to handle and terminate, as the conductor consisted of stranded steel which went everywhere. This in turn had to be connected to the Army telephone called Tele F which was a robust iron affair with a handle generator. These cables were then connected to the road wires back to the Wareham Telephone Exchange where they were cross connected to the Lytchett cables and thence to the Gun Operations Room. There were normally three men operating the anti-aircraft site at Arne which was a round the clock operation. The men occupied tented accommodation on the site.

In late 1941 the Post Office commenced discussions with the military authorities regarding the communication requirements of the invasion forces but, unlike more leisurely peace-time provision, the whole scheme had to be carried out in complete secrecy. Swanage was chosen to have two communication links installed for D-Day, whenever that came. The town was one of the strategic landing points chosen for submarine cables from the Cherbourg area. As well as this, as way of a back-up and in case the submarine cable failed or was destroyed, a site on Godlingston Hill was chosen for a vital high frequency radio link to Normandy.

I was told that I must not say anything to anybody in Swanage about the work I was doing, not even at home to my mother, father or family. This was quite normal and was repeated to me every time I was given a job, 'You do not mention this to anyone'. All I was told was that it was connected with D-Day, and that if I looked at Godlingston Hill in the morning, I would know before anyone else whether the invasion was going to take place, because I would see the aerial lifted. I therefore knew it was going to be a radio link associated with D-Day.

The bunker at the base of Godlingston Hill

The bunker took the form of deep excavations dug into the base of Godlingston Hill overlooking Knitson Farm. The equipment comprised land line terminals, amplifiers for the long distance lines, a switchboard, and a means of cross-connecting any of its radio or land circuits. The accommodation was extensive and consisted of several buried interconnected Nissen huts reinforced with bricks and concrete and covered with soil and turf. Kitchen and toilet facilities were provided along with an apparatus room and diesel electric powered standby equipment. The diesel generator was situated in a room about twenty feet square off the apparatus room but this certainly wasn't sound-proofed. The engineers from HQ arrived one day to carry out noise level tests on the circuits, but someone else was test running the diesel at the time! A Royal Signals man was operating the switchboard which was in narrow room on the left. The technical Signals staff had been trying to start the diesel without success, but one day the switchboard operator pointed out to them that the oil level was at zero: once that was pointed out they were at last able to start it!

The equipment was delivered by van which came up a track through Knitson Farm. I remember the delivery quite clearly because it was raining at the time and the delivery man didn't want this delicate equipment wet and said "Come on you lot, get your raincoats off and cover the equipment". I didn't bother! The equipment was installed by the Royal Corps of Signals. My part was to check in all the equipment and install a standard Post Office switchboard. Underground cables had been brought to the site and these were connected to the switchboard to provide private wire direct communications to three Combined Operations Headquarters which were being built at Plymouth, Portsmouth and Dover. Lines to the signal centre at Southampton were also included while Dover was earmarked as an invasion embarkation point solely as a deception plan to mislead the Germans.

The lines from Godlingston Hill went underground and were then cut into the Swanage to Wareham cable. Three cables were used between Wareham and Swanage at that time, so they had to cut into a cable with spare wires to send it down to Wareham telephone exchange, this had a large frame so they could then be pushed off to the different places with amplifiers.

The aerial at the top of Godlingston Hill was fixed to a hinged base and laid flat on the ground for security reasons; this was to be erected on D-Day. Near this aerial was another bunker which housed a collection of individual radio transmitters and receivers for the particular communication needs of each armed service on D-Day, mainly Army and Navy. They were probably operated by staff familiar with using the equipment every day in conjunction with others of a similar service group at the far end. The Navy had a very tall wooden mast, made of two stout telephone poles joined together to obtain the double height; these were then set in a concrete foundation. There was quite a little forest of aerials on small, inconspicuous masts, one for each transmitter/receiver. I think each service there staffed its own equipment.

It was later arranged for me to meet with Dr. Lewis (an expert from Post Office Headquarters) to provide basic assistance if required while he tested and commissioned the whole installation. The site at the base of the hill was eventually staffed out by the Royal Corps of Signals prior to D-Day, whose staff I believe, were billeted locally.

In late 1942 work commenced on the installation of a number of submarine terminating points for communication with Normandy. The Royal Navy, Signals Units and the GPO worked together in laying and landing these cables.

The first was a fairly local one, it was laid underground from the Godlingston site to a point just below the Grand Hotel and thence via submarine cable to Southbourne. It's purpose was to provide an alternative routing for the Godlingston-Normandy radio link in case the land lines via Wareham should suffer damage. At Southbourne the cable was extended to an underground amplifier station situated where the Tuckton Bridge roundabout now stands. Cables and equipment there gave access to the main trunk cable network where the circuits were extended to the command centres.

The second and major submarine cable was to prepare for a secure and more long term link to the advancing forces in France, once a land foothold had been established, to replace the short term radio facilities provided for the seaborne attack.

Two cables were laid by Post Office cable ships from a point near the Mowlem to a few miles off shore at Querqueville near Cherbourg. The cables would then be landed soon after D-Day, when hopefully the Cherbourg area would be cleared.

Swanage was chosen because it was the shortest distance from Cherbourg for a cross-Channel submarine cable system, but technology at the time could only cater for the cable length from Cherbourg to Swanage and amplilfication was required in order to extend to the main GPO network at Wareham and Southbourne,

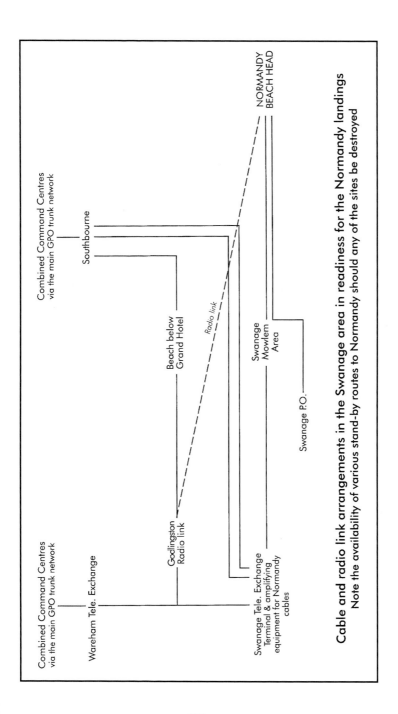

Cable and radio link arrangements in the Swanage area in readiness for the Normandy landings
Note the availability of various stand-by routes to Normandy should any of the sites be destroyed

so the shore ends of the cables were extended, one to the first floor of the old Post Office in Station Road which was to be used as a back-up, and the other in an underground duct to the Telephone Exchange in Locarno Road. Here the special amplifying equipments for the cables were installed. They were then extended back via the Mowlem and the sea to Southbourne where they were sent on via the trunk network to the various command centres. This was to be the primary communication route for the British forces following the Normandy landings.

I learned later that, on D-Day, cables from Swanage which had been laid to points near the French landing sites were seriously damaged by ships dragging their anchors in a gale. A few days after the landings the cable ship 'Monarch' was sent to pick up the damaged cable from Swanage to complete the connection to shore.

Swanage telephone exchange in wartime

In pitch darkness they were hit by shells which they thought came from shore but in fact turned out to be 'friendly fire'. The 'Monarch' was sunk close to shore but refloated some time later.

Records show that the Godlingston Hill-Normandy radio link was fully operational on D-Day plus one, and was possibly the only line of communication available to the British forces during the first few days of the Normandy landings.

Early in 1943 it had been thought that the possibility of a German Commando raid on this part of the coast could not be ruled out. It was therefore decided to station a Home Guard contingent armed with sten guns in the Swanage Telephone Exchange. This was provided on a twenty four hour basis by small groups working in

A Morris Minor GPO van used during the war

shifts. One of the corporals in charge was Charlie Reynolds an ex-army Sergeant Major from the First World War. He was a single man who lodged in the New Inn in the High Street and joined the Home Guard when war broke out.

Probably my closest shave in Swanage was when I was on the 7.10am Swanage-Wareham train on April 20th 1942; I was going to work in Wareham. The train was just pulling out of the station when we became aware that the latter was being attacked by aircraft, and heard machine gun fire. The train however just kept going and no one aboard was injured. The raid was all over in seconds. When we arrived at Wareham and disembarked we could see bullet holes on the top of some of the carriages. Later we heard that there were fatalities in Swanage and that Montague Purchase's shop had been bombed. We knew something important had happened because the Wareham switchboard became congested.

I spent quite some time at the Wareham exchange and sometimes used to listen to the messages that were coming in from aircraft to the advance station on Studland Hill. I was able to do this because I was involved in laying the circuits through Wareham to wherever they were going, in this case RAF Middle Wallop. After they were installed I checked to see that they were all working correctly. I can distinctly remember conversations going on between our fighter pilots while they were in dog-fights, with a number of 'tally-hos' going on!

In April 1943 I was called up into the navy and went into the Fleet Air Arm. I was sent to Warrington and there I did testing for apprenticeships. I did reasonably well in my tests and checks because of my background, and having been to college. I was then transferred into the Royal Navy as an electrical artificer. I worked on acceptance testing on new ships that were being launched, and among these was H.M.S. Vanguard, then the largest battleship in the world; it was built in John Brown's shipyard, Glasgow. I went backwards and forwards to Glasgow with an ordnance artificer while the Vanguard was being built, to test the various electrical equipment. The Vanguard was built mostly by women. I would go down into the hold of the ship and would tap a welder on the shoulder only to discover it was a Scotswoman! There were far more women building the battleships and destroyers at this time than there were men. I can remember on one occasion going down the river to Greenock and counting twenty eight destroyers in the process of construction. We had a phenomenal capacity to build in those days, and get things done.

When I was demobbed and returned to live in Swanage, my Post Office work continued, but I was sent to the Bournemouth area to work as a special faults investigator.

Wesley Mullen

Wesley came to Swanage as part of the American 1st Infantry Division, the 'Big Red One'. He stayed eight months and was billeted in the north of the town. On D-Day his Company landed on Omaha Beach.

Wesley Mullen by the Millpond in 1944

I arrived in Swanage in October 1943 as part of the build up of forces for the D-Day landings. I was in the 26th Regiment, 2nd Battalion, G Company, 2nd Platoon, and was a rifleman.

I was billeted in a house in Ulwell Road with our platoon of about forty men and we stayed there for the whole duration of our stay. We slept on fold-up beds and there was a small fireplace in each room where we burnt what we could to keep us warm in winter. Our food station was the Grand Hotel and we all walked up there for our meals. The hotel was used by the US military for billeting our officers and possibly one platoon of soldiers, along with our cooks.

Whilst in Swanage we did very little training at all, but on occasions we would go on a five mile march. While we were in town there was one air raid that I can remember. When we heard the plane we ran outside, which was not the smartest thing to do; a single bomb was dropped behind the house we were in and machine gunned some of the vehicles that were around. As far as I remember there were no casualties.

The 3rd platoon outside their billet at 14 Burlington Road, now the Bella Vista Hotel

Our leisure time was substantial since we did very little training. In the evening we would wander down the town, stop off at the local pubs for a beer and then go and buy some fish and chips at the shop at the bottom of Court Hill. When we got a pass at the weekend we usually went over to Bournemouth to go to a restaurant or to the theatre.

The highlight of the week was going to the dance at the Gilbert Hall in Kings Road. The music was supplied by members of our military band who played Glenn Miller music. It was good because we didn't have to pay to get in, but the one drawback was that the mothers of the girls attending sat in the balcony to keep an eye on things. When the dance finished the mothers waited at the exit to make sure that their daughters didn't leave with any GIs. I found this rather amusing since, if young people want to meet up with one another, they usually find a way of doing so.

The lovely time soon ended and our company left Swanage around 1st June 1944 to travel to Portsmouth for embarkation to boats for the D-Day landings. Our destination was the dreaded Omaha Beach. The 1st Division was made up of three regiments: the 16th, 18th and 26th, I was in the 26th as a rifleman.

We embarked into LCIs (Landing Craft Infantry). These were flat bottomed boats that could carry one infantry company (250 men). These boats were comprised four compartments with two ramps at the bow for direct landing on the beach. Our 2nd platoon occupied the second compartment.

Our LCI headed for Omaha Beach on 6th June 1944. The 16th regiment was the first to land at daybreak and sustained 90-95% casualties and the 18th landed next with 50%; the casualties were enormous. We approached the beach but became stuck on a sandbank. We had to transfer immediately to two smaller landing craft which could each hold about forty five men. We then headed for the beach and landed about noon. My most vivid recollection of that day was that when the front ramp was dropped, we were constantly pushing bodies aside in the water to reach the shore. Because of the enormous sacrifices of these earlier landings we were able to land quite easily with very few casualties.

2nd platoon outside 17 & 19 Ulwell Road our billets, now the Tower Lodge & Beachway Hotels'.

We crossed the beach and went up the embankment overlooking the Channel. Upon reaching the top four other men and myself were directed to take a patrol to contact the 29th Regiment which was to our left. The message we received was to move to their left and close the gap between the 1st and 29th divisions. When we returned our company headed inland. For seven days we had no food and very little sleep until we came to Caumont-l'Éventé about twenty miles inland, which I believe was the furthest penetration of the beach-head.

At one time during the crossing of France our 2nd platoon was ambushed resulting in twenty four being killed, six wounded and eight surviving. I was one of the lucky ones.

I wanted to say I would never forget my time spent in Swanage and the kindness shown by all the people I came into contact with. I only hope that some day I will get back to thank you all.

Swanage in the 1920s & 1930s

by Stewart Borrett

Eleven contributors share their personal accounts of life in the town. The accounts clearly show how the town came through the depression years far better than most, largely due to the two week holiday in Swanage being taken very seriously.

Published 2002. 75 pages with photographs, priced £7.50